LEARN
CHESS
QUICK

LEARN CHESS QUICK

By Brian Byfield & Alan Orpin. Illustrated by Gray Jolliffe.

BATSFORD

First published in the United Kingdom in 2010 by
Batsford
10 Southcombe Street
London
W14 0RA

An imprint of Anova Books Company Ltd

ISBN 978 1 906388 66 9

A CIP catalogue record for this book is available from the British Library.

18 17 16 15 14 13 12 11 10
10 9 8 7 6 5 4 3 2 1

Reproduction by Spectrum Colour Ltd, Ipswich
Printed and bound by 1010 Printing International Ltd, China

This book can be ordered direct from the publisher at
the website www.anovabooks.com, or try your local bookshop.

Distributed in the United States and Canada by Sterling Publishing Co.,
387 Park Avenue South, New York, NY 10016, USA

Cartoons hand coloured, using the TRIA system by LETRASET

www.letraset.com

Contents

INTRODUCTION

This book has been written on the assumption that the reader agrees with one or all of the following notions:

1. Chess is about as exciting as watching grass grow.

2. Children who play Chess are terrifyingly intelligent, wear glasses and get very high marks in maths.

3. Chess is another way of saying 'I hate you'.

If these are the sort of things you think, don't worry. Twelve out of nineteen people feel exactly the same way, and not one of them has played Chess in their life.

Yet strangely enough, in spite of the widespread belief that Chess is all a bit nerdy, it's still by far and away the most popular game on earth.

In Russia, for instance, practically everybody plays Chess. It's their national game.

As far as the rest of the world is concerned, thousands of new players are getting hooked by the minute, just as they have been for centuries.

We'd like you to be next, and what's more, we think you will be.

But be warned… once you realise what an utterly simple but totally fascinating game it is, you'll be a goner.

And once you've discovered what it really feels like to grind your opponent into the ground, you'll realise that it's a rush that you can't live without.

Chess will scare the pants off you at times. It will certainly make you angry. It may possibly cause you to visit the toilet more frequently than usual and it might even give you a big head.

But one thing is for sure.

It will never bore you. Not ever, ever.

This book will teach you everything you need to know as a complete beginner.

It will start, not surprisingly, with the rules. And they aren't as frightening as you might think.

It will introduce you thoroughly to each individual piece and show you exactly how they operate.

It will give you some basic tips that will remain invaluable to you for as long as you play Chess. Stuff like what is generally good, what is generally bad, and what is downright suicidal.

And finally it will introduce you to a range of violent tactics that in real life would land you in jail for a very long time.

What it WON'T do is confuse you with the mind-boggling subtleties of advanced Chess.

Above all, the book is an attempt to illustrate the simple magic of the game. To bring it alive, not kill it stone dead with unnecessary complex theories.

Work through it systematically, playing out the examples we'll be showing you, and very soon you and the kids will be wondering why you never learned to play earlier.

Remember, every great Chess player was a beginner once.

Even if it was only for about half an hour.

THE BASICS

The Game

The object of the game is definitely NOT, as many people think, to kill off all your opponent's men. In fact it's theoretically possible to win without taking a single piece.

The enemy King is your ultimate target and to win the game you have to work out a dirty, merciless plan to trap the fat old fool like a rat.

When you've achieved that, you've 'Checkmated' him.

Being 'Checkmated' is absolutely not a pleasant experience.

We recommend you avoid it at all times.

The Board

There is very little you need to know about a chessboard.

It consists of 64 Black and White squares. And it should always be placed so that a White square is in the bottom right hand corner.

The lines of squares that run from left to right are called 'Ranks'.

The lines of squares that point straight up the board at the enemy are called 'Files'.

And the lines of squares that run diagonally in any direction are called 'Diagonals'.

That is all.

Except of course, that a chessboard is a very violent place.

If you have a weak stomach, you should never go on one.

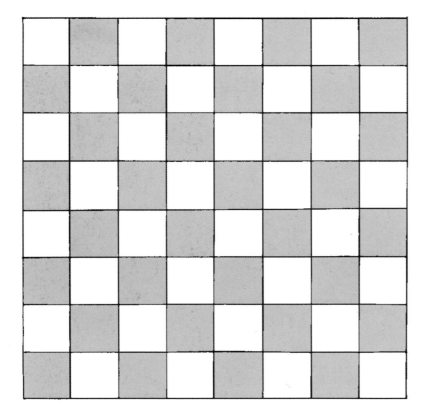

The Pieces

Each player's army consists of 16 men. Or to be a little more accurate, 15 men and one lady.

There are 8 Pawns, 2 Knights, 2 Bishops, 2 Rooks (sometimes called Castles), a Queen and a King.

In our diagrams, they will always be shown in the following way:

Pawn   Knight   Bishop   Rook   Queen   King

There is only one rule to remember about setting up the pieces and that is QUEENS ALWAYS GO ON THEIR OWN COLOUR.
In other words, in the starting positions, the White Queen must always be on a light square, and the Black Queen on a dark square.

Set them up now and study the scene. Terrifying, isn't it?

To start a game, they are laid out like this:

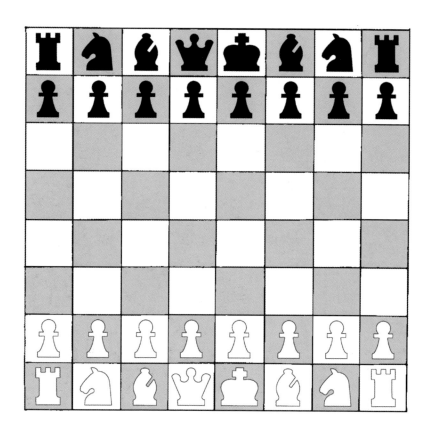

The Pieces. Treat them right and they'll be your friends for life.

Although there are 32 pieces on a chessboard, the great thing is, you only have to learn how to move six of them.

Let's start with the Pawn…

The Pawn

In everyday language, the word 'Pawn' has come to mean 'Sucker' or 'Stooge' – someone who's happy or dumb enough to do everyone else's dirty work.

In Chess, there's no doubt that Pawns do a lot of the dirty work. They have no choice – they're the Front Line, and 99.9% of the time it's a Pawn that sticks his head above the trenches and makes the first move in a game.

But when they're asked to die, they win medals and pave the way for the big guns waiting behind.

Individually, they're the weakest pieces on the board because the way they move and capture is very restricted.

But in groups they can do permanent damage, and in defence they're magnificent. There's nothing worse than having a nice-looking plan messed up by a well-organized bunch of Pawns in front of you.

Unfortunately, because of their size, Pawns often don't get the respect that their tiny boots deserve. They get sacrificed meaninglessly or left to stagnate.

Beginners are often too eager to start a scary-looking march up the board with the bigger pieces, only to watch them getting hacked to pieces a few moments later.

Resist this temptation. It won't get you anywhere. Big pieces make big targets.

Instead, be patient. Get your Pawns moving slowly but surely in the early stages and TAKE CONTROL OF THE CENTRE OF THE BOARD.

Be a good Pawn player and you'll be a good Chess player.

How the Pawn moves.

Unlike your other pieces, Pawns can only move forwards.

They have a one-way ticket to the far reaches of the battlefield.

And on the way there, they must do, or be done.

When they're moving (not capturing), they advance ONE SQUARE AT A TIME. DIRECTLY AHEAD.

There's only one exception to this rule, and it's very easy to remember.

All eight Pawns have the choice of moving one square ahead or two squares ahead, but ONLY ON THEIR FIRST MOVE.

After that, they are limited once again to one square.

Whether you move them one square or two squares on the opening move is up to you.

Experience will tell you which is the best step to take.

If an enemy piece is camped on the square directly ahead, that's just too bad. The Pawn must wait till the road clears.

A PAWN CANNOT JUMP OVER OTHER PIECES.
FRIEND OR FOE.

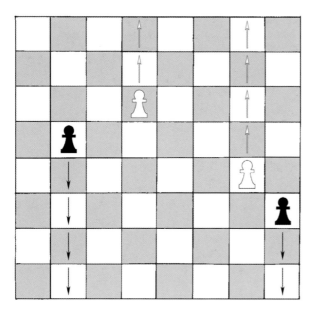

Fig 1. The Pawn advances one square at a time directly ahead.

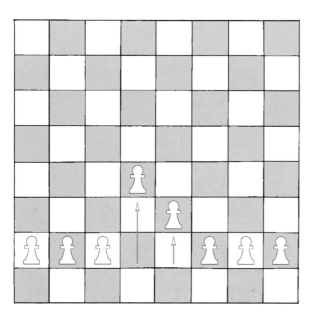

Fig 2. But on its opening move ONLY, a Pawn can move one or two squares.

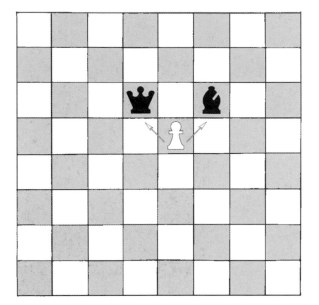

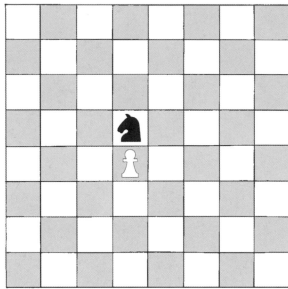

Fig 3. The Pawn captures one square diagonally to the left or right. Here the Pawn can take either the Queen or the Bishop.

Fig 4. A Knight blocks its path. The Pawn has nowhere to go.

How the Pawn captures enemy pieces.

Although Pawns move one square directly ahead, they capture ONE SQUARE DIAGONALLY AHEAD. TO THE LEFT OR RIGHT.

In this respect, they're different from all the other pieces. Because, as you will shortly discover, every other piece captures the same way it moves.

To capture an enemy piece, the Pawn simply moves one square diagonally left or right, and removes the piece that's camped on that square.

When is a Pawn not a Pawn?

When it's a Queen. Or a Rook. Or a Bishop. Or a Knight.

Confused? Here's the explanation:

When a Pawn survives long enough to reach the 'Rank' at the far end of the board, a huge reward for his courage and cunning awaits him.

The rules allow him to turn into any piece he wants except a King.

This is called 'Pawn Promotion', and when it happens it's seriously bad news for your opponent.

The beauties of such a delicious moment are discussed later in the book.

In the meantime, never forget that inside every Pawn there's a Queen trying to get out.

The Knight

Unlike all the other pieces on a chessboard, the Knight is a double act. He does his job on horseback.

This also allows him to do something that the others can't do.

He can move and capture round corners. What's more, he can attack and capture enemy pieces even when there are other pieces in the way.

He can jump over pieces, friend and foe alike.

He can even threaten eight pieces at the same time.

This makes him not just sneaky, but very dangerous. When your Knights are on the rampage, your opponent won't know whether he's coming or going. (Usually he'll be going).

If the Knight does have a weakness, it's his mobility. He can't move around the board with the ruthless speed of a Queen or Rook or Bishop. He's a bit slow, as you're about to find out.

And for that very reason, here's a tip you should never forget:

GET YOUR KNIGHTS ON THE MOVE *EARLY*.

How the Knight moves.

In Fig 1, you see all the squares that the Knight can move to from the square he's on. How he gets to any one of those squares looks a bit complicated, but really it isn't.

The simplest way to figure out where he can go next is to remember the L shape.

And that L shape is always made by either:

a) Moving 2 squares sideways and 1 square up or down,
b) Moving 1 square sideways and 2 squares up or down,
c) Moving 2 squares up or down and 1 square sideways,
d) Moving 1 square up or down and 2 squares sideways.

Before you give yourself a severe headache trying to take all that in, practise it now on the board until you get the hang of it. And note how those instructions tie in with Figs 1 and 2.

It doesn't matter how you arrive at the squares in Fig 1 & 2 as long as you apply the all important 'L' shape.

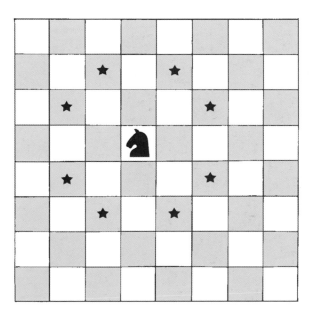

Fig 1. The Knight can move to any of the starred squares from the square he's on.

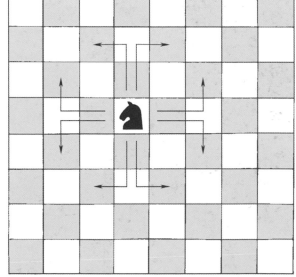

Fig 2. He gets to the squares by moving in a 'L' shape.

How the Knight captures.

In this respect, the Knight is the same as all his buddies except the Pawn.

He captures the same way as he moves.

In Fig 3, the Knight will capture the Bishop next move. Notice that he can do this even though a Pawn seems to be in the way. He can jump over the Pawn. Remember, A KNIGHT'S PATH CAN NEVER BE BLOCKED BY ANY PIECE. HIS HORSE SEES TO THAT.

In Fig 4, you are looking at a very beautiful thing.

The Black Knight is in a position to take his pick of any of the 3 fat White pieces that are within his range.

And not one of them can do anything about it.

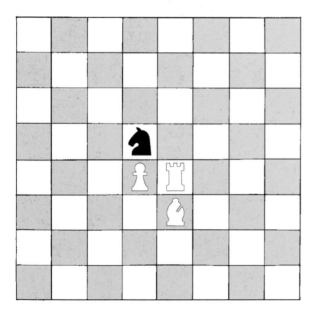

Fig 3. A Knight's path can never be blocked by any piece. Whether he's moving or capturing. Here he can take the Bishop.

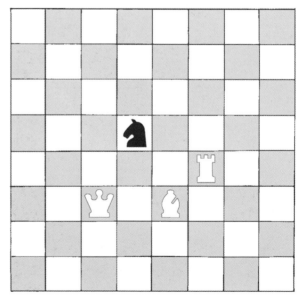

Fig 4. The Knight can capture the Queen, the Bishop or the Rook.

The reason is obvious. They can't get at him because they all move in straight lines.

And there stands the Knight, cool as you like, lurking just around the corner from all of them.

This is called a Fork. So called because of its double – or in this case triple – pronged attack.

The beauties of Forking and the horrors of being Forked are further discussed in a disturbing little section beginning on page 92.

And there you have the Knight. Slow, dangerous, cunning, mysterious.

A cross between Attila The Hun and Don Quixote.

The Bishop

You may perhaps think of Bishops as harmless old gentlemen with a smile for everyone and a complete lack of fashion sense.

On a chessboard, Bishops don't wear hoods, they ARE hoods.

Their idea of a perfect Sunday is a bloodbath, hiding behind pawns, threatening members of the opposing Royal Family and then moving silently in for an orgy of merciless, long-range killing.

This may surprise you given their present place in society, but the fact is that centuries ago when the game was invented, most Bishops were rated by the number of people they'd burnt at the stake, and their role as assassins on a chessboard therefore came as no surprise to anybody.

On your board, think of them as Terminators for the Almighty, mobile as snakes in an oil drum and able to cover a lot of ground in one move.

For this reason, it's usually wiser during the early stages of the game to give your slower pieces, like the Pawn and the Knight, a chance to get moving before you produce your Bishop.

But don't hold him back too long. Look for early opportunities to do a bit of PINNING. This has nothing to do with dressmaking, and you can see why in the section starting on page 86.

One final point: Although the Bishop and the Knight are considered to pack the same degree of attacking punch, Bishops are far better to have around during the Endgame when only a handful of pieces are left on the board. This is because, dangerous as they are, Knights take time to get anywhere.

How the Bishop moves.

The Bishop moves along the Diagonals. AND ONLY THE DIAGONALS.

He can move as many squares as he likes, or as few as he likes. Backwards or forwards. HE CANNOT MOVE AROUND CORNERS.

In Fig 1, you can see all the squares the White Bishop could move to from the square he's on. Eleven in all.

Notice that in your army, you have two Bishops.

One operates up and down Black Diagonals, the other operates up and down White Diagonals.

If you should ever discover that both your Bishops are on the same colour squares, something is wrong.

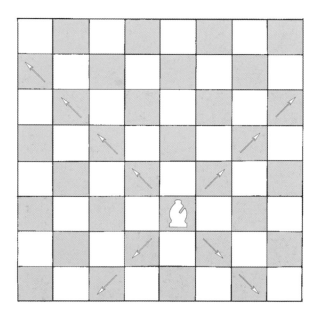

Fig 1. The White Bishop could move to any one of the arrowed squares.

How the Bishop captures.

The Bishop captures the same way that he moves. He can pick off any enemy piece unfortunate enough to be camped on the same Diagonal. (That's assuming there are no pieces in the way.)

BISHOPS CANNOT JUMP OVER OTHER PIECES.
FRIEND OR FOE.

To capture, the Bishop moves to the square the enemy piece is camped on, and removes it from the board.

In Fig 2, the White Bishop could capture the Black Queen, Rook or Bishop. He can't take the Black Knight. The White Pawn is in the way.

N.B. Prayer has so far proved ineffective when enemy Bishops are on the rampage.

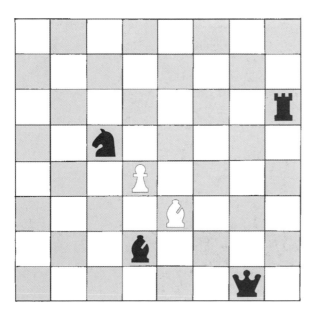

Fig 2. The White Bishop could capture any one of the three Black pieces. He can't capture the Knight, his Pawn is blocking the way.

The Rook

In your army, you have a couple of cool dudes called Rooks. Dark name. Dark intentions.

Individually, their taste for blood is bettered only by the Queen.

But you only have one Queen.

You have two Rooks. And as a pair of psychopathic twins they add up to the most powerful attacking force on the battlefield.

Together is how they operate best.

At the start of the battle, the rules demand that they're separated by the full width of the board, so they have to stand around and mutter impatiently.

But later on, when clear space has opened up between them and they're able to join forces, they start doing the biz. (There's a neat, legal trick that speeds up this process, called 'Castling'. See page 60)

Once together, an open file is what they like best. In other words, a straight line of squares that's been cleared of pieces from one end of the board to the other.

This is the chink in the enemy's armour they've been waiting for.

And when they're travelling up it you can hear those Royal knees begin to knock.

And that's the first and most important tip to remember about your Rooks.

1. ROOKS WORK BEST ON OPEN FILES. SO START LOOKING FOR WAYS OF OPENING SOME.

2. DON'T WASTE A LOT OF TIME TRYING TO GET YOUR ROOKS OUT TOO SOON. YOU'VE GOT FAR MORE IMPORTANT THINGS TO DO EARLY ON IN THE GAME.

Their time will come.

3. ALWAYS, IF POSSIBLE, GET YOUR ROOKS WORKING TOGETHER, EACH ONE BACKING THE OTHER ONE UP.

4. Finally, ROOKS DON'T ALWAYS WORK BEST IN THE CENTRE OF THE BOARD, LIKE MOST OF THE OTHER PIECES.

SNEAKING UP THE SIDE OF THE BOARD IS ONE OF THEIR NASTIEST TRICKS.

How the Rook moves.

The Rook moves in straight lines. Up and down Files. Or along Ranks. He can move backwards or forwards. Or sideways in either direction. As many squares as he likes, or as few as he likes.

THE ONLY THING A ROOK CAN'T DO IS JUMP OVER OTHER PIECES OR MOVE DIAGONALLY.

In Fig 1, you see all the squares the Rook could move to from the square he's on. Fourteen in all. And notice that wherever he is on the board, he always has 14 possible squares to move to.

This is a trick possessed by no other piece.

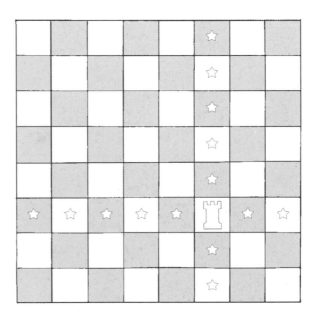

Fig 1. The Rook could move to any one of the 14 starred squares.

How the Rook captures.

The Rook captures the same way that he moves.

In Fig 2, the Rook has the choice of capturing any of the four White pieces camped around him.

But notice that he can't capture the White Knight, because that would mean moving diagonally, and that he can never do.

To capture an enemy piece, he simply moves to the square that the enemy piece is camped on, and removes it from the board.

And that was the Rook. Oh, and his ugly brother.

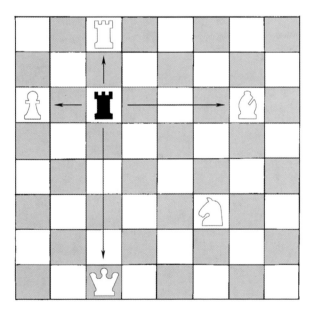

Fig 2. The Black Rook could capture any one of the four White pieces. He can't capture the Knight, as he lies on a Diagonal.

The Queen

The King may be the most important piece on the board, but it's his wife who wears the trousers.

The Queen is a monster in a frock.

Ladylike? Not a chance – she's a book-definition control freak and a born killer.

She can throw her weight around like no other piece on the board.

Along Ranks and Files like a Rook, and up and down Diagonals like a Bishop. In one giant step she can travel the length or breadth of the battlefield.

But beware. Big pieces also make juicy targets, so resist the temptation to send her off on lone missions early on in the game.

Bring her out too soon and suddenly you could find yourself wasting valuable time defending her. She may be screaming to get on with it but don't listen to her – listen to us…

Be strong.

Just say: 'No, dear.'

How the Queen moves.

In Fig 1, you see all the squares the Queen could possibly move to from the square she's on. Twenty-seven in all.

Up and down Files. Across Ranks. Up and down Diagonals.

As many squares as she likes. Or as few as she likes.

In fact she can do just about anything she wants except move round corners like the Knight and jump over other pieces.

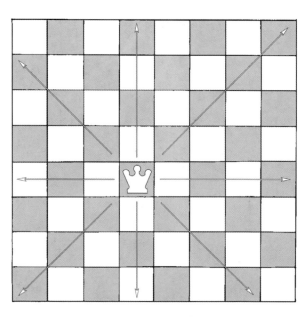

Fig 1. The Queen can move to any of the squares covered by the arrows, one square at a time or in one sweeping movement.

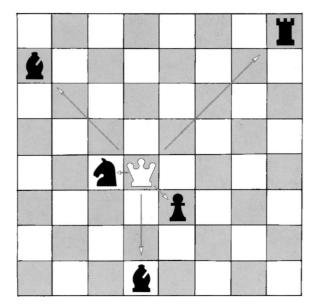

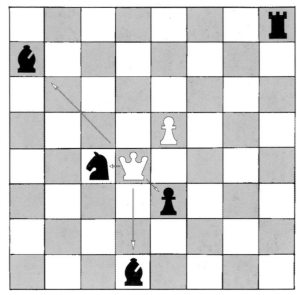

Fig 2. The White Queen could take any of the five Black pieces in her sights.

Fig 3. Now the Queen can take only 4 of the 5 Black pieces. Not the Rook, because her Pawn is blocking the way.

How the Queen captures.

In Fig 2, the White Queen could capture any one of five Black pieces.

Notice that some of them are quite a long way from her while the others are right next to her.

To capture any one of them, she moves to the square the unfortunate piece is camped on, and removes it.

In fact, she captures the same way as she moves.

The King

For someone with such a powerful title, the King is surprisingly weak.

He's quite content to do as little as possible, leaving everyone else to carry out the dangerous business of winning his battles..

Have we heard that somewhere before? We think we have…

Usually, the only time you'll see a King showing any kind of energy is when he's got a bunch of well-organized thugs on his tail, at which point he has no choice but to hitch up his robes and run as fast as his flabby little legs will carry him.

This, by the way, is not fast at all. Kings can only move one square at a time.

Do not forget, however, that the King is ultimately the most important character in the game. Every single move your opponent makes, no matter how subtle, is in some way an attempt to bring the King to his knees.

He is the object of all the aggression dished out by the enemy, and he must therefore be protected at all costs.

He should never figure in your plan of attack during the early or middle stages of the game.

Not only is he too weak to do any real damage, but including him in the rough stuff would bring him out into the open.

Would you send your grandpa downstairs to see off the burglars instead of your beefy marine-corps brother?

Exactly.

In the early stages of the game, you can do no better than build yourself a solid attacking position up the centre, and by so doing, protect your King at the same time.

There is one extremely effective method of building a protective wall around your King early in the game, and that's called 'Castling'. You can learn all about it in the next chapter, but basically, it allows you to tuck your King away in a heavily defended corner.

How the King moves.

As we've just explained, the King is a bit of a weakling.

He can only move one square at a time. In any direction. Forwards, backwards, sideways, diagonally. The only exception to this rule is when the King is Castling.

In Fig 1, you see all the squares the Black King could move to from the square he's on. Eight in all.

Not much of an athlete, is he?

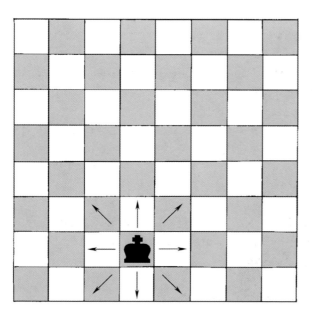

Fig 1. The King could move to any one of the eight squares next to the square he's on.

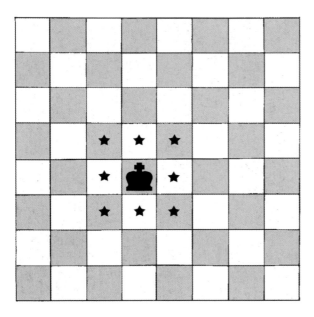

Fig 2. The King could capture any piece one square away from him in any direction.

How the King captures.

The King captures the same way that he moves.

He can take any enemy piece that happens to be in one of the eight adjacent squares around him.

In Fig 2, we've only shown you the squares that are in the King's attacking range.

If we had shown the King surrounded by 8 pieces, although they would certainly all be within his range, the King could not take any of them because if he did, he would immediately put himself in 'Check'. What it means to be in Check is fully explained in a later chapter.

When you have read it, you will immediately understand the problems of illustrating Fig 2.

For now, all you need to know is that the King captures the same way that he moves.

And to do that, he moves to the square that an enemy piece is camped on, and removes it from the board.

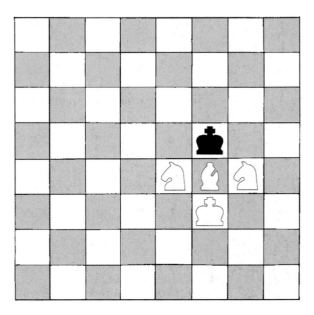

Fig 3. The Black King can't capture any of the White pieces on the Rank in front of him. By doing so, he would wind up right next to the White King, and this is illegal.

Why rival Kings can never see eye to eye.

For obvious reasons the Black King doesn't think much of the White King, and vice versa.

As a result, they don't like getting too close to each other.

Because of this, THE TWO KINGS CAN NEVER BE NEXT TO EACH OTHER ON ADJACENT SQUARES. It's one of the rules of the game.

In Fig 3, you'll see what we mean.

If the Black King were to take any one of three White pieces in front of him, he would wind up on a square immediately adjacent to the White King.

But this is illegal.

All three White pieces are safe.

Can kings ever be captured?

No.

They must stay on the board until one of them has been battered into submission.

How chess games are recorded

Anyone who's lived through a war knows what war correspondents do.

They're the brave reporters, always in the thick of the action, writing it all down for the folks back home.

Unfortunately, the system of recording Chess can never have quite the excitement of "As I stand here, the shells are bursting all around me…" but it does have the advantage of allowing folks all over the world to relive Chess battles exactly as they happened in the safety of their own home.

Quite apart from that, it would be impossible to teach or learn Chess unless such a system existed.

Nowadays, the most commonly used system is called Algebraic Notation.

It sounds complicated but, in fact, it's really very simple.

Algebraic notation

Here is the board with the algebraic notation co-ordinates.

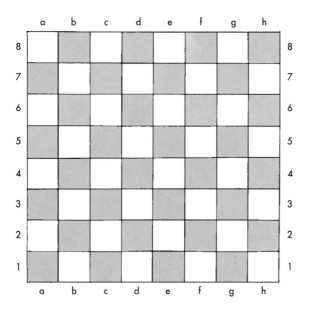

The Files going up the board are the letters a, b, c, d, e, f, g, h.

The Ranks going across the board are numbered 1, 2, 3, 4, 5, 6, 7, 8.

So each square can have its own name.

Because each square has its own name it's easy to describe a move.

It may look like a nightmare but, in fact, it's perfectly straightforward and very logical.

For instance, from our grid we can work out that the White Queen will start the game on d1. And the Black Queen will start on d8.

The eight White Pawns prepare for battle lining up along the 2nd Rank from a to h.

Set up the pieces and check it out.

	a	b	c	d	e	f	g	h	
8	a8	b8	c8	d8	e8	f8	g8	h8	8
7	a7	b7	c7	d7	e7	f7	g7	h7	7
6	a6	b6	c6	d6	e6	f6	g6	h6	6
5	a5	b5	c5	d5	e5	f5	g5	h5	5
4	a4	b4	c4	d4	e4	f4	g4	h4	4
3	a3	b3	c3	d3	e3	f3	g3	h3	3
2	a2	b2	c2	d2	e2	f2	g2	h2	2
1	a1	b1	c1	d1	e1	f1	g1	h1	1
	a	b	c	d	e	f	g	h	

Just to make sure you've got the hang of it, where is the White Rook?

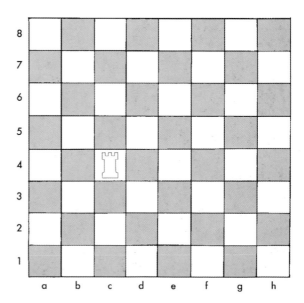

The Rook is on the c File.
The Rook is on Rank number 4.
So the Rook is on c4.

Where is the Black Knight?

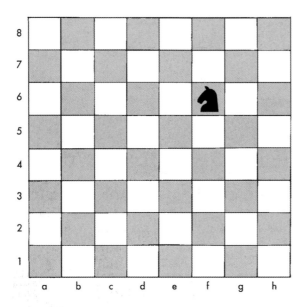

The Knight is on the f File.
The Knight is on Rank number 6.
So the Knight is on f6.

Now let's see the letters and symbols we use for the pieces.

Piece	Letter	Symbol
KING	K	♔
QUEEN	Q	♕
ROOK	R	♖

Piece	Letter	Symbol
BISHOP	B	♗
KNIGHT	N	♘
PAWN	P	♙

You may have spotted that Knight doesn't begin with a N. It's nice to know you're paying attention. But a N is used for the Knight so as not to confuse it with the King.

And when recording a Pawn move, you only write down the square on which the Pawn lands – there is no need to precede this with the letter 'P'.
All you need to know now is that the moves are recorded in order. White always goes first.

Now we can start to write down the moves of the game. Let's start from the beginning. White has opened 1. d4 and Black replies 1. …Nf6.

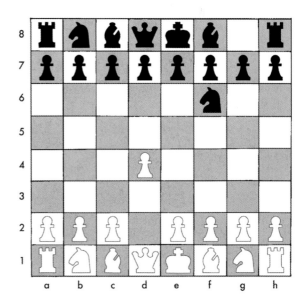

So that's how we write it down. 1. d4 Nf6.

One last point. In our diagrams, in fact in all Chessboard diagrams, White will always be at the bottom attacking 'upwards' and Black will always start at the top attacking 'downwards'.

This is a universal system. All Chess books use it. And so do newspapers and computers.

Now, what do we write when a piece is captured?

To make sure you've completely understood the system of recording the Chess moves that we've just been through, set the pieces up in their starting positions and play out the following moves:

1. e4	e5
2. d3	d6
3. Nf3	Nc6
4. Be3	Nf6
5. Nc3	d5
6. e x d5	N x d5
7. N x d5	

If your battlefield looks like this, you've completely got the hang of it. If it doesn't, you've made a mistake. So go through the moves again as many times as it takes to get it right.

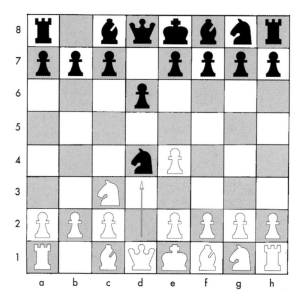

The White Queen captures the Black Knight. It is written down Q x d4.

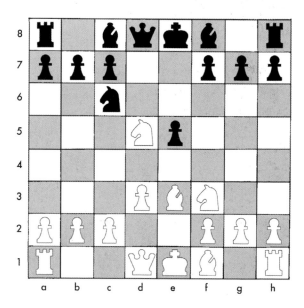

PLAYING THE GAME

Being in check

When you're in Check (written down as +), it means that your King is under direct attack from an enemy piece, and would be taken next move if he stayed where he was.

But, as Kings can never be captured and removed from the board (except at the end of the game when they've been Checkmated), something else has to happen. The King must get himself out of Check.

1. He can move to any adjacent available square that isn't under attack from an enemy piece.

2. He can place one of his own men right in the line of fire to block the attack.

3. He can capture the offending piece either with one of his own men, or all by himself.

There are also various ways that he can't get himself out of Check.

1. He can't Castle out of Check. He can't Castle ACROSS Check either. Or of course Castle INTO Check.

2. He can't capture the offending piece with one of his own men if moving that man means revealing himself to Check from another enemy piece. (This is called a Pin. And it's so nasty that we've devoted a whole section to it on page 86).

3. The King can't capture the offending piece if it means that he'll still be in check after he's done it.

ONE MORE POINT. THE KING CAN NEVER MOVE TO A
SQUARE THAT WOULD PUT HIM IN CHECK, WHETHER HE'S
CAPTURING OR NOT.

When you're in Check, when do you have to get out of it?

Immediately.

Unfortunately, this means that you'll just have to abandon any sinister
plans you may have had for carving holes in your opponent's defence,
and start doing a little defensive work of your own.

Of course, being in Check doesn't necessarily mean that you're in big
trouble. Very often, by moving one of your own pieces to block the
attack, your opponent finds himself under attack and has to beat a
rapid retreat.

So remember. Don't put your opponent in Check just for the hell of it.
Wait until it causes him some real problems.

In every game there's a tipping point, a time to strike. A time when one
decisive move turns the tide of the battle. You'll get to sense the right
time to make this move. Sometimes it's just a pawn moved forward a
square. Whatever it is, remember Checkmate is your objective.

What's worse than being in Check?

Being in Double Check. And that means you've got big problems.

By simply moving one piece, your opponent has put you in check from two different directions.

Moving one of your own pieces to block the attack won't help. It can only deal with one of the Checks.

THERE IS ONLY ONE WAY TO GET OUT OF DOUBLE CHECK. YOUR KING HAS TO MOVE.

The Double Check is a lethal weapon. You can read more about it on page 110. And that's what being in Check is all about.

Not a very pleasant section, was it?

Checkmate

And now for the moment you've all been waiting for. Checkmate.

At the beginning of the book, we explained that the object of the game was to trap the enemy King like a rat. To Checkmate him (written down as #).

So this is what Checkmate is all about.

Quite simply, a King has been Checkmated when an enemy piece moves, puts the King in Check, and the King has no way of getting out of it.

Any move he could possibly make, any square he could possibly move to, would still leave him in Check.

Very often when this happens to you, you'll immediately start searching for ways of crawling to safety.

It will take you a moment or two to go through all the possibilities, and then suddenly the awful truth will dawn on you.

Checkmate.

You've lost.

It's very, very unpleasant when your opponent does it to you.

But when you do it to him, it's just plain magnificent.

By the way, it's considered rude to say 'Check' very loud (unless it's directed at your Dad), but inside your head you can shout and scream as much as you like.

We show here four examples of Checkmate. Notice that in all of them, no matter where the King tries to go, he still remains in Check. And he can neither move a piece to block the attack, nor capture an enemy piece to ease the situation.

Painfully simple.

And now a word of warning.

During the actual play, beginners often think that Checkmate has happened when in fact it hasn't.

So, when you think it has, go through the following routine:

Take the King that's apparently been Checkmated, and try out ALL the possible moves that are open to him.

Then, see if moving a piece would block the attack. (Making sure that by moving that piece, you don't reveal the King to Check from another direction.)

Finally, make sure that the enemy piece that's doing the Checking can't be taken, either by the King himself, or one of his army.

When all the possibilities have been exhausted and you know you've lost, you're now free to go away and sulk.

But if you've won, you're fully entitled to be unbearable for an hour or so.

What Checkmate looks like.

It doesn't look too bad. But it feels awful.

Any move the Black King could make to escape the White Rook's Check would still leave him in Check.

Note that the Black Bishop can't move to block the Check. It would reveal his King to Check from the White Bishop (see Fig 1, below).

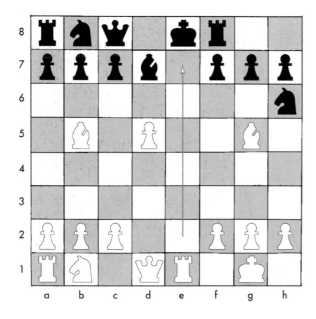

Fig 1. Checkmate. Because the Black Bishop cannot defend the King.

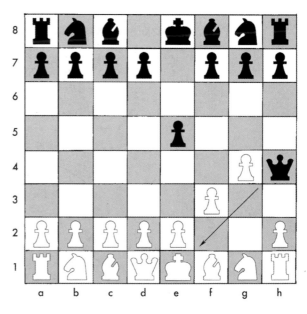

Fig 2. Checkmate. The King has no defence.

The White King has nowhere to run (see Fig 2, below left). And not one of his pieces can block the Check from the Black Queen. CHECKMATE! A silly two-move game by White.

No wonder it's called Fool's Mate. It's the only way a game can end in two moves.

White to move.

1. f3   e5
2. g4   Qh4 # Checkmate

The Black King can't move and the White Knight can't be taken. Checkmate. Black has used his 2 Knights very badly. With one of his, White has won the game (see Fig 3, below).

Although both sides have the same amount of pieces, the White King has a headache which proves to be fatal. Checkmate (see Fig 4, below).

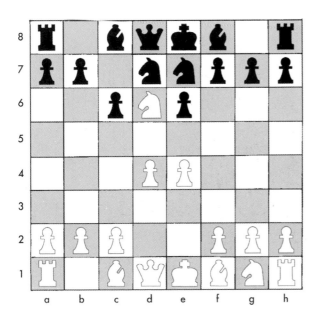

Fig 3. Checkmate. The King is surrounded by his own pieces.

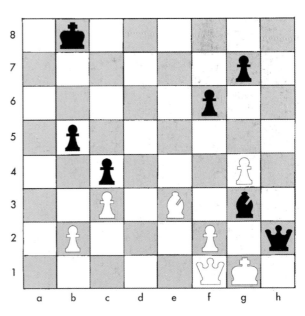

Fig 4. Checkmate. The Black Queen has trapped the White King.

Stalemate

Just because the King can't make a move, it doesn't mean you can

Stalemate is probably the worst thing that can happen to a game of Chess.

It means that you've just spent the last hour and a half racking your brains for nothing.

In other words, a draw.

Stalemate is not an agreed draw, a situation where you and you opponent decide that neither player can win and consequently call the whole thing off.

There are definite rules that govern it.

And here they are:

1. You are limited to King moves only. You may very well have a handful of men left on the board, but for one reason or another, they can't move, or aren't allowed to move.

2. Your King is not in Check.

3. It's your move.

4. Any move your King could possibly make would land him in Check.

Now you may be thinking that this set of conditions looks remarkably like Checkmate.

But it isn't. And the big difference is in rule No. 2: 'Your King is not in Check'.

If he was in Check, and any move he could possibly make would still leave him in Check, then that of course would be Checkmate.

Fig 1 is a Stalemate situation. Notice that none of the Black pieces can move.

Only the Black King can move. And either of the squares available to him would put him in Check.

There are times when Stalemate is better than nothing. Particularly when you're losing and victory for you is out of the question.

That is the time to start manoeuvring towards a Stalemate position.

Your opponent will hopefully be far too occupied with Checkmating you with his overwhelming positional superiority to even consider that you've got a nasty shock in store for him.

In fact, maybe Stalemate isn't such a waste of time after all.

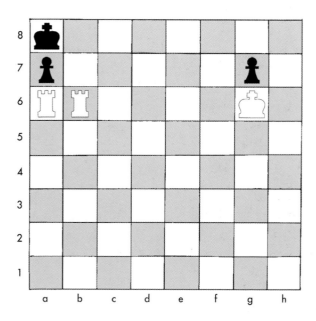

Fig 1. Black to move. The Pawn on a7 can't take the Rook because the King would be in Check, so none of the Black pieces can move, except the King. He's not in Check now, but any of the moves open to him would land him in Check immediately. Stalemate.

Perpetual Check

Perpetual Check, like Stalemate, is another way that a game can end in a draw, even though one side looks certain to lose.

As you can imagine, it's worth a try if your situation is looking hopeless.

In Fig 1, White is a whole rook down. Normally, he wouldn't stand a monkey's chance of drawing the game.

But in this position, with White to play, he manages to pull it off. Thanks to the Perpetual Check rule.

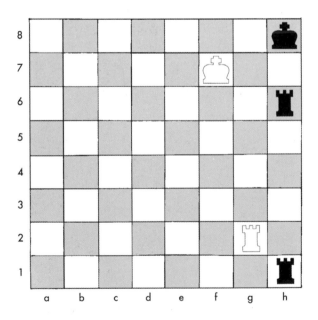

Fig 1. The White Rook moves to g8, Checks the Black King, and Perpetual Check is a foregone conclusion.

And here's how he does it.

First, the White Rook moves to g8 and Checks the Black King.

The Black King can't block the Check with any of his men, and he can't capture the White Rook either, because by doing that, the Black King would wind up on a square immediately adjacent to the enemy King, and that's illegal.

So the Black King has to move. And there's only one square he can move to. h7.

At this point, White will breathe a sigh of relief if he's got a brain in his head, because he'll see that the only possible outcome is a draw by Perpetual Check.

And here's White's next move. Rg7. Check.

When it's happened 3 times, White can claim a draw, because this backwards and forwards business is just going to go on forever.

In fact, the rules that cover Perpetual Check state that if the exact same position is reached THREE TIMES during a game, either player can claim a draw.

Just to fully understand the moves we've just been through, here they are again.

Play them out now, and you'll understand what Perpetual Check means.

1. Rg8+   Kh7
2. Rg7+   Kh8
3. Rg8+   Kh7

And so on and so forth till you're blue in the face. It's a draw, folks, it's a draw.

The lesson to be learned from this is that you've never actually lost until you've actually been beaten.

Castling

Castling is one of the most important things you can do in a game of Chess. Particularly in the early stages of the battle.

In a single move, you can shift your King into a highly fortified defensive position and, at the same time, get one of your Rooks out into a strong attacking position.

It's the only time in Chess when two pieces can be moved in one move.

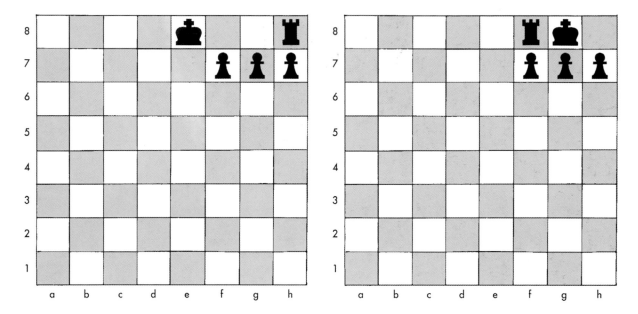

Fig 1. The King and the Rook are now ready to Castle on the King side.

Fig 2. This is what it looks like when they have.

When can you Castle?

As we've just pointed out, the Castling move involves the King and the Rook. NEVER ANY OTHER PIECES.

In Fig 1, the Black King and the King-side Rook are in the correct position for Castling.

Notice that there are no pieces between them. This is important.

In Fig 2, Black has Castled. And this is how it happened.

First, the Black King moved TWO SQUARES SIDEWAYS and arrived at the square next to the Rook.

Then, the Rook jumped over the King and landed on the square on the far side of the King.

Practise that now. It's very straightforward. And look at the result.

The King is no longer wide open to an attack down the centre. He's tucked away behind a wall of Pawns in the corner.

Anyone who tries to get at him in that position is going to wind up with a few broken bones.

And the Rook, instead of being bottled up behind the Pawns, is suddenly out in the open and ready to practise his evil habits.

How many ways of Castling are there?

Two. We've just showed you one.

The other way still involves the King and the Rook, but this time it's a different Rook.

The Queen-side Rook.

In Fig 3, the King and the Rook are in the correct position for Castling.

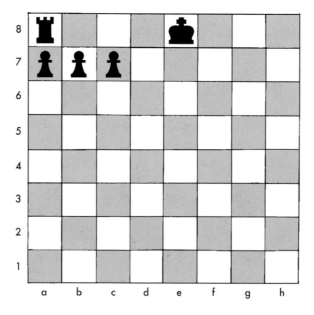

Fig 3. The King and the Rook are now ready to Castle on the Queen side.

Once again, there are no pieces between them.

Only this time, you'll notice that they're one square further apart.

So this is what happens.

As before, the King moves two squares sideways towards the Rook. And although this doesn't bring him directly alongside the Rook, the Rook still jumps over the King and lands on the square on the far side of him.

In Fig 4, you see the result of Queen-side Castling. Notice how the final position differs slightly from King-side Castling.

When Chess games are recorded, King-side Castling is written down like this: 0-0 (sometimes called Castling short).

Queen-side Castling is written down like this: 0-0-0 (sometimes called Castling long).

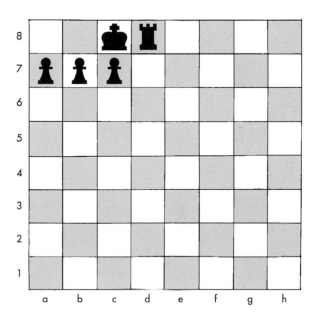

Fig 4. This is what it looks like when they have. Notice how the final position differs slightly from the Kingside Castling.

Which way of Castling is better?

Neither. It all depends on how the battle is shaping up. If, for instance, it looks like your opponent is launching a full-scale attack on your King side, then obviously you'd Castle into safety towards your Queen side. And vice versa.

But don't forget that one of the main objects of Castling is the protection of your King. So if the defensive (usually Pawn) cover on the side you want to Castle is weak, it may be better not to Castle at all.

You will learn with experience when to Castle, when not to, and which is the better side to Castle to.

When is Castling illegal?

Quite often.

In fact, there are four different occasions when Castling is not allowed.

Being obscenely rich I have two castles – but which one shall I move?

First, there must always be a clear path between the King and the Rook he'll be Castling towards.

So, IF THERE ARE ANY PIECES BETWEEN THE KING AND THE ROOK, YOU CAN'T CASTLE.

Second, you can only Castle when the King and the Rook you plan to Castle with haven't made a single move during the game up to that point.

It may happen that the King makes a move off his starting position, and then moves back again to that square later on. Although the position may then look correct for Castling, it isn't.

So, IF THE KING OR THE ROOK YOU PLAN TO CASTLE WITH HAS MADE A MOVE, CASTLING IS ILLEGAL EVEN THOUGH THEY MAY HAVE MOVED BACK INTO THE CORRECT POSITION FOR CASTLING.

Third, you can never Castle out of Check. In other words, YOU CAN NEVER USE CASTLING AS A WAY OF GETTING OUT OF CHECK. Sorry, but you'll just have to find some other way of doing it.

Fourth, YOU CAN NEVER CASTLE ACROSS CHECK. This means that if in the act of Castling, the King has to pass over a square that's under attack from any enemy piece, then you can't Castle.

And of course, THE KING COULD NEVER CASTLE INTO CHECK.

Remember these four rules. There are always big arguments about them when beginners are playing.

When is the best time to Castle?

Because of the millions of different variations that can crop up during a game of Chess, there are obviously no hard and fast rules about when to Castle and when not to.

But as a beginner, if you want to build yourself a sound offensive as well as defensive position, then the expert says this: CASTLE EARLY. This usually means some time around your tenth move. It should always be part of your plan, so don't delay getting your Knights and Bishops out of the way and on the move.

Of course, if you've got your opponent on the run, then don't go blindly following this rule. You could waste a very important attacking move.

But if the battle looks pretty even, then Castling is one of the best moves you can make.

How much is each piece worth?

Obviously, the Queen is worth much more than the Pawn.

But how much?

And how much more valuable would you say a Rook was than a Knight?

To help give you a reasonably accurate picture of how much each piece is worth, the following scale has been worked out.

The Queen – 9 points   The Bishop – 3 points
The Rook – 5 points   The Pawn – 1 point
The Knight – 3 points

You could also see it as a Knight being worth 3 Pawns. Or a Queen being worth 3 Bishops or 9 Pawns.

The King doesn't have a value. Maybe that's because he's priceless.

Now this point system has nothing to do with the outcome of the game. If you take your opponent's Queen, it doesn't mean that you've scored nine points.

It's only there to give you a quick indication of how you stand.

If during a game, you opponent has captured a Knight, two Pawns and a Rook, his bag amounts to 10 points. And if you've taken two Rooks, a Pawn and a Knight, your bag would amount to 14 points.

In this situation, you could reasonably assume that you were on top.

But don't let yourself be carried away if your points tally is much bigger than your opponent's.

It doesn't necessarily follow that you're going to wind up by slaughtering him.

Your position might be desperate. Your King might be hopelessly hemmed in. Even though you have many more pieces left on the board than he does.

The point system also teaches the beginner not to go fishing round the board taking a Knight if it means losing a rook in the process.
You'll soon learn to appreciate the real value of each individual piece.

Starting the moment your opponent takes your Queen with one of his Pawns.

The En Passant rule

How a Pawn can capture another Pawn without really capturing him.

A long time ago, Pawns didn't have the choice of moving one square or two squares on their opening move.

They were restricted to one square only.

This meant that the game took rather a long time to get moving.

So it was decided that in the interest of earlier bloodshed, all Pawns should be allowed the choice of moving two squares off their starting positions.

This also meant that in certain situations, particular Pawns would have an unfair advantage over their opposite numbers.

So, to even things up a little, an equally unfair rule was introduced.

The En Passant rule.

Living proof that two wrongs make a right.

En Passant is French for 'in passing'. We will now explain how the rule works.

In Fig 1, it would seem that the Black Pawn has come to a dead end for the time being.

He can't advance straight ahead because of the White Pawn directly in front of him.

And he doesn't have anything to attack.

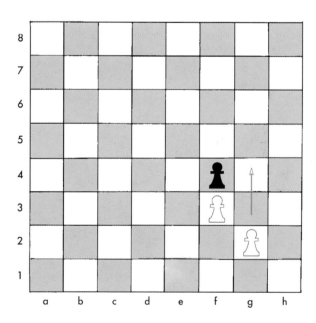

Fig 1. The White Pawn moves 2 squares ahead off his
starting position. He looks safe...

In this innocent-looking position, the White Pawn on g2 thinks he's got it made.

Obviously, he wouldn't move to g3 as he would immediately be taken by the Black Pawn.

So he decides to exercise his option of moving two squares off his starting position, and arrives alongside the Black Pawn in what he thinks is a safe position.

Not only is he feeling pretty smug about getting out of danger, but he reckons he's managed to get right past the Black Pawn and out into the open as well.

Unfortunately, this White Pawn has a very short memory.

He's forgotten about the En Passant rule.

And here comes the bombshell.

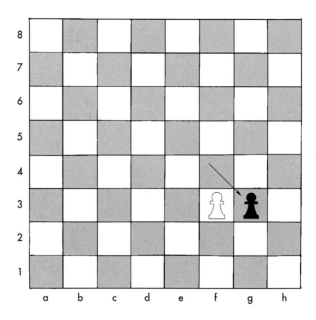

Fig 2. ...but he's not. The Black Pawn immediately takes him EN PASSANT.

By moving diagonally to g3, the Black Pawn takes the White Pawn 'in passing'.

In Fig 2, you'll see what's happened.

Now, the way the Black Pawn took the White Pawn in the situation we've just been through doesn't tie up at all with what we've previously taught you about the Pawn.

But don't let that bother you. Just remember the following rules:

1. THE EN PASSANT RULE ONLY APPLIES TO ONE PAWN TAKING ANOTHER.

2. It can only be used IMMEDIATELY AFTER the Pawn advancing TWO SQUARES off his starting position has made his move. If for instance in Fig 1, the White Pawn moved alongside the Black Pawn, and the Black Pawn chose not to take him En Passant next move, he would have missed his chance. The Black Pawn would not be allowed to take the White Pawn on any subsequent moves.

Practise it now.

To be honest, the En Passant situation doesn't arise too often. And for this very reason, it can catch you out in a big way when it does.

So don't say we didn't warn you.

Pawn promotion

In real life, conspicuous bravery in the armed forces is usually rewarded with medals and, in some cases, film contracts.

In Chess, outstanding acts of Pawn heroism are rewarded with extremely rapid promotion.

It all happens when a plucky little Pawn manages to duck and weave his way right to the far end of the battlefield and reach the 8th Rank.

As you know, Pawns can never retreat, and they certainly can't move too quickly either.

All of which makes it very difficult for a Pawn to survive long enough to ever reach the 8th Rank.

But it does happen, particularly towards the end of a game when there aren't too many pieces left on the board.

And when it does, these are the consequences.

The moment a Pawn arrives on the 8th Rank, he must weigh up the situation and decide which piece he wants to be promoted to.

Remember, HE CAN'T REMAIN A PAWN. AND HE CAN'T BECOME A KING.

He must then be immediately replaced by the piece he has decided on. (Usually, you'll be able to use a piece that was captured earlier on in the game. But if the right piece isn't available, an upturned Rook is the recognized way of getting round it.)

The Pawn becomes a Queen.

In most cases, the obvious thing for the Pawn to do is turn into the most powerful piece on the battlefield, i.e. the Queen. (This may seem a little unnatural, seeing that Pawns are all men, but that's the way it goes.)

And, incidentally, the fact that you may still have your original Queen on the board doesn't matter. Now you have two. You could have three if you wanted.

If you can't turn that into a quick victory, there's something very wrong with the way you're playing.

In Fig 1, it's White to move. The White Pawn on the 7th Rank will capture the Black Rook, and by doing so, arrive on the 8th Rank.

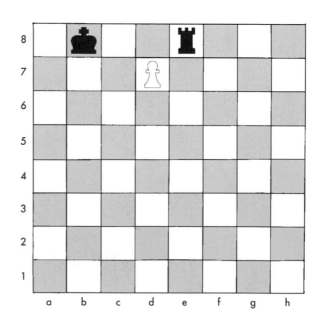

Fig 1. White to move. The White Pawn will capture the Black Rook next move, and by doing so he'll become a Queen.

He then immediately becomes a Queen. ON THE VERY SAME MOVE.

In Fig 2, look what's happened. By becoming a Queen, the White Pawn has put the Black King in Check. THE BLACK KING MUST THEREFORE GET OUT OF CHECK IMMEDIATELY.

So to sum up Figs 1 & 2, here once again is what happened. The White Pawn on the 7th Rank captures the Black Rook, arrives on the 8th Rank, turns into a Queen, and puts the Black King in Check. ALL IN ONE MOVE.

In Fig 3, you see almost the same thing about to happen all over again. But this time, the White Pawn has only to move one square ahead to reach the 8th Rank. There's no Black piece to capture, but he can still become a Queen.

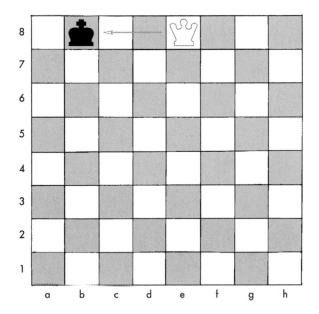

Fig 2. As the Pawn is now a Queen, the Black King is immediately put in Check.

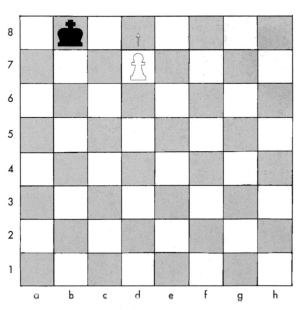

Fig 3. The eighth rank is undefended, and the pawn moves forward to promotion.

Why is it sometimes better not to become a Queen?

That question can be best answered by looking at Fig 4. Although Black is about to lose a Rook to the White Pawn, there doesn't seem to be any immediate threat to the Black Queen or the Black King once the White Pawn has reached the 8th Rank.

And that is where you're so wrong.

You automatically assumed that the White Pawn would become a Queen.

Well he doesn't. He becomes a Knight. Immediately putting the Black King in Check. An extremely beautiful move.

And because the Black King must use his next move to get out of check, White will take the Black Queen next move. You can see how it happened in Figs 5 & 6.

The lesson to be learned from this is that when one of your Pawns reaches the 8th Rank, don't go blindly assuming that he should become a Queen. Look around to see if there are any more violent possibilities. The one we've just shown you is a classic.

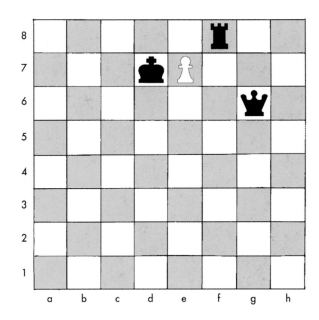

Fig 4. White to move. This time, the White Pawn captures the Black Rook and becomes a Knight. Wow.

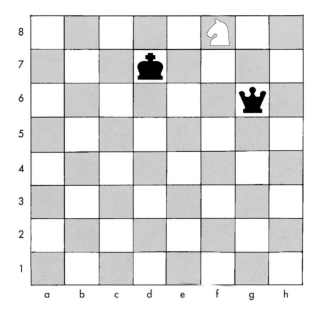

Fig 5. The Black King is now in Check from the White Knight, and must use his next move to get out of Check…

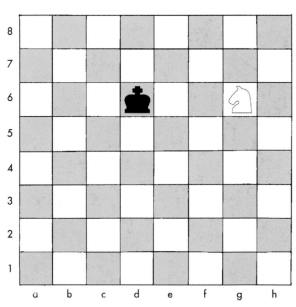

Fig 6. …And the Knight takes the Black Queen next move. Delightful. Let's have a big hand for that White Pawn.

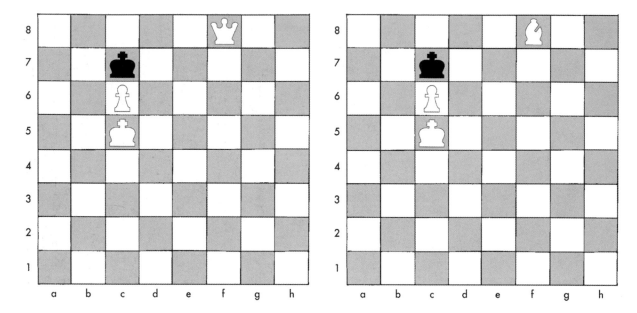

Fig 7. A White Pawn has mistakenly become a Queen.
The Black King can't take the Pawn, and can't put himself
in Check. Stalemate. The Pawn was dumb.

Fig 8. A White Pawn has now wisely become
a Bishop, avoiding a Stalemate position.

When is it sometimes better to become a Bishop or a Rook?

You may very well think that because the Queen is a combination of
the Bishop and the Rook in the way that she moves and captures,
promoting one of your Pawns to a Bishop or a Rook is a waste of time.

Sometimes, it isn't.

Because sometimes, promoting your Pawn to a Queen will immediately
lead to a Stalemate position.

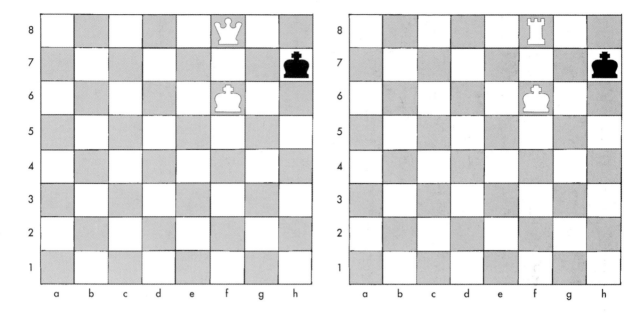

Fig 9. A White Pawn once again makes the mistake of becoming a Queen. The Black King has nowhere to go. Stalemate.

Fig 10. A White Pawn has correctly become a Rook. The Black King can move. No Stalemate, and Black will be Checkmated next move.

In Fig 7, the White Pawn mistakenly becomes a Queen, and Stalemate follows next move.

In Fig 8, the Pawn has this time correctly become a Bishop.

in Fig 9, the White Pawn has once again made the mistake of becoming a Queen, and Stalemate follows immediately.

In Fig 10, the Pawn has become a Rook. No threat of Stalemate, but a definite threat of unbearable pressure on the Black King.

Aren't Pawns powerful?

Why chess players often go blind

Have you ever spent hours looking for something, like your car keys, finally given up in desperation, and then realised that it was sitting right under your nose all the time?

The same thing happens in Chess.

You spend a long time meticulously figuring out your next move. You decide that it's a good one and you make it.

And then WHAM. You watch in total disbelief as your opponent calmly takes your Queen.

The really infuriating thing is that your opponent's obvious next move was staring you in the face.

But for some reason you never saw it.

Now if this sort of thing happens to you, and it most definitely will from time to time, don't go thinking that you're some kind of a dummy.

It happens to the best of us.

And we really mean that.

There are many famous instances of top international Chess masters making absolutely dreadful blunders during important tournaments.

And nine times out of ten, their only excuse was 'I never saw it'. Slightly worrying when you consider the degree of concentration Chess masters are capable of.

Keep your eyes open.

Unfortunately, there are no guaranteed methods of getting blunders out of your system.

But there is a very simple way of making sure they don't happen too regularly.

Every time it's your move, CHECK EACH OF YOUR PIECES TO MAKE SURE THEY'RE NOT UNDER ATTACK.

Also, MAKE DOUBLE CERTAIN THAT ONCE YOU'VE DECIDED TO MOVE A PIECE, YOU HAVEN'T LEFT IT WIDE OPEN TO IMMEDIATE CAPTURE. (Unless of course you're making a deliberate sacrifice.)

Only when you're absolutely sure that the coast is clear should you make your move. Famous last words.

Why some experienced chess players pretend to be blind.

What we're about to tell you would almost certainly be frowned on by many Chess experts. But it's fun, so who cares?

Very often, you make a move and immediately realise it was a huge mistake. This is usually followed by a groan of dismay and a thumping of the forehead with the palm of your hand.

Your opponent will undoubtedly see this.

And will waste no time in punishing you for your mistake, normally by taking the piece you've just moved.

Now there are times when you have a plan that calls for a deliberate sacrifice of one of your pieces.

And it's vital to the plan that your opponent immediately takes the piece you've offered him.

So here's what you do.

Move the piece, pause, and then groan with phoney dismay and thump your forehead with the palm of your hand.

Your opponent will automatically assume that you've blundered, and will take your piece, falling nicely into your trap. With any luck, he will then realise the error of his ways, groan with dismay and start thumping his forehead with the palm of his hand.

We hope you liked that.

Enough excuses – how did you miss that fork?

Why the centre of the board is important.

Imagine you're in a boxing ring. And your opponent's got you pinned up against the ropes. Life doesn't look too promising, does it?

You've only got one place to run to. The centre of the ring. And to make matters worse, your opponent knows it. So he's waiting for it.

You should be in the centre, Sire – I can't tell them you're in the bog

And when you do, he's going to bop you.

Now, if you were standing in the centre of the ring already, you'd have a hundred per cent better chance of survival. Because you'd have a whole lot more room to dodge about in.

Exactly the same thing applies to Chess.

In attack as well as defence, the centre of the board will usually help you, while the edges of the board will usually slow you down. We can demonstrate this simply and dramatically.

In Fig 1, the White Queen is in the centre of the battlefield and is commanding no less than 27 squares.

On the other hand, the Black Queen is way over to the side, commanding only 21.

In Fig 2, the White Knight has 8 possible squares to move to while the Black Knight has only 4.

Naturally, the same thing applies to the Bishop. But not to the Rook.

While all other major pieces thrive in the centre of the board, the rook can do major damage sneaking up and down the sides getting behind the enemy lines.

There is also another reason why the centre of the board is important.

If you can take undisputed control of it with a very strong formation of pieces, it not only puts up a big barrier for your opponent to get through, but also provides an excellent launching pad for your own attacks.

If you remember this, you'll be a very difficult player to beat. If you don't, you'll make a very enjoyable opponent.

Because a lot of people are going to have a ball thrashing you.

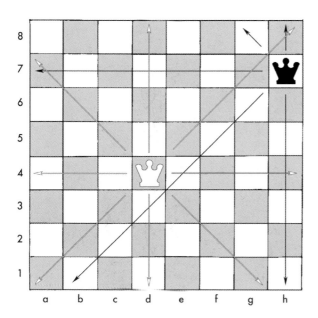

Fig 1. The White Queen covers 27 squares, while the Black Queen in the corner covers only 21.

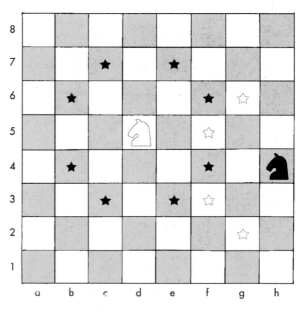

Fig 2. The White Knight in the centre covers 8 Black Stars. Whereas the Black Knight on the side of the board can only command the 4 White ones.

TRICKS

Now that you've learned how all the pieces move, here are some particularly nasty tricks you can pull with them.

By this stage, you know how all the pieces move and capture. You've been given a few sound hints. And you know all the rules of the game. So theoretically, you're ready to play real Chess.

Even if you didn't bother to learn any more about the game, as long as you're enjoying it, it doesn't matter a hang whether you're a good player or not.

But then, how many people would want to be mediocre players forever? Not many.

So from now on, you're going to learn what it takes to be a good player. And it's going to be a lot of fun.

In fact, the rest of the book is devoted to that most delightful of all Chess aspects, VIOLENCE.

The first seven sections cover the Pin, the Fork, the Skewer, the Discovered Attack, the Discovered Check, the Double Attack and the Double Check.

All of them are simple to learn. All of them will make you a more feared opponent. And all of them will help you plan your attack.

They'll give you something to aim at, rather than stumbling along in the dark hoping that something will eventually turn up.

We can promise you that once you've learned the basic principles of these seven tactical devices, defence will never be one of your strong points.

Possibly due to lack of practice.

The Pin

Have you ever dreamed that some ghastly thing was creeping towards you and for some strange reason you were rooted to the spot?

If you have, you're already a long way to understanding what a Pin is.

Look at Fig 1. And notice that the Black King, the Black Knight and the White Queen are all in a straight line on the same File.

The Black Knight is powerless to move. Rooted to the spot.

And this is why. If the Black Knight moved, he would immediately expose his King to Check from the White Queen. And this, as you already know, is illegal.

The result? The Black Knight will be taken next move by the White Queen. And there isn't a thing he can do about it.

Always remember that PINNED PIECES ARE PARALYSED PIECES. And for that reason, they make excellent targets. They can't fight back.

Look at Fig 2.

The Black Rook is pinned against his King by the White Queen. He can't move away from that square without exposing his King to Check.

It's White to move. And he moves his Pawn one square forward. Immediately attacking the Rook.

Normally, the Rook would be able to move away from the Pawn's threatened attack. But this time he can't because of the Pin.

He must stand there, bound hand and foot, and allow himself to be captured by the Pawn.

Just like in the nightmare.

We now show more examples of the Pin. And not only that, but also how to set up a Pin situation.

Learn them well. And remember the Golden Rule. WHEN YOU'VE PINNED AN ENEMY PIECE, ATTACK IT.

It can never run away.

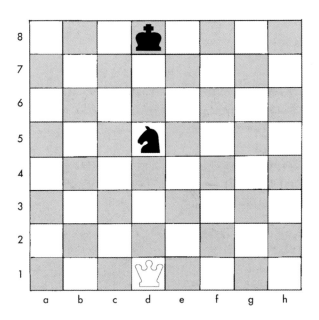

Fig 1. If the Black Knight moved, he would immediately expose his King to Check from the White Queen. The Knight must stay where he is. He's Pinned and will be captured by the Queen next move.

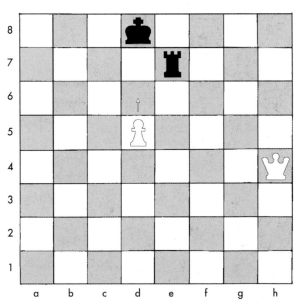

Fig 2. The Black Rook is Pinned to his King by the White Queen and can't move. Rooted to the spot, he's at the mercy of the White Pawn.

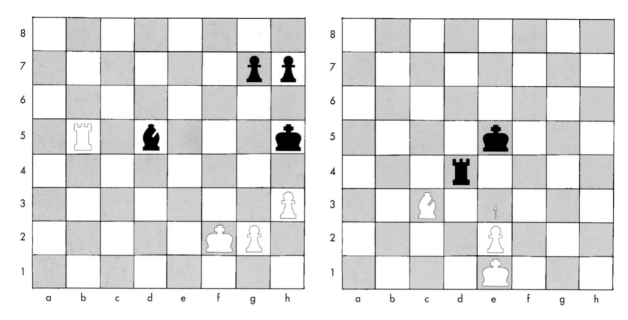

Fig 3. The Black Bishop cannot move. He is at the mercy of the White Rook.

Fig 4. The Black Rook is pinned by the White Bishop. The pawn makes its move.

Black to move. The White Rook paralyzes the Black Bishop by pinning it against the Black King. The Bishop is undefended and will be taken by the Rook next move (see Fig 3, above).

White to move. White could exchange his Bishop for the Black Rook. But he doesn't. Instead, he attacks the Pinned Rook with his Pawn. And gets it for nothing (see Fig 4, above)!

White to move. White, in a desperate situation, spots one of the tell-tale signs of a possible Pin. Black's King and Queen are in a straight line on the same File! But first, he must remove the Black Pawn. So here goes (see Fig 5, below):

1. R x g7 + !!

Black to move. Black must relieve the Check by dealing with the Rook. Realistically, he only has two choices:

1. ...K x g7   or   1. ...Q x g7

In both cases, the King and Queen will still be left in a straight line, so White plays:

2. R g1 and Pins the Queen against the King. The Queen is lost (see Fig 6, below).

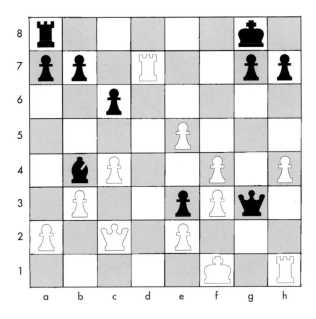

Fig 5. By checking with the White Rook on g7, White spots a potential pin.

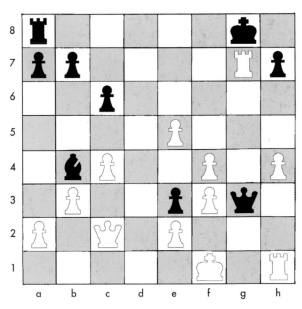

Fig 6. Black has only two choices. Both will lose the Queen.

Black to move. The White Queen looks bogged down. Here's what happens (see Fig 7, below):

1. …Q x g2 + !
2. Q x g2   R x e2

In Fig 8 you can see what's happened.

White to move. The White Queen is in big trouble. Pinned by the Black Bishop, she can't take the threatening Black Rook. Her only way out is to commit suicide and take the Black Bishop with her like this:

3. Q x c6   b7 x c6

The deadly Pin has worked wonders for Black. He's 2 Pawns ahead, as well as having Rook for Bishop and bound to win (see Fig 8, below).

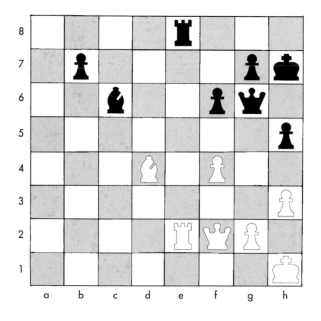

Fig 7. The Black Queen sees an opportunity on g2.

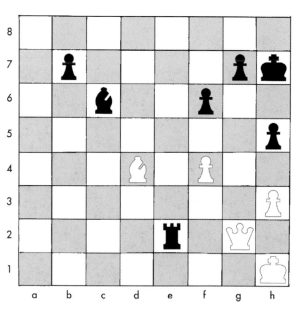

Fig 8. The White Queen is lost.

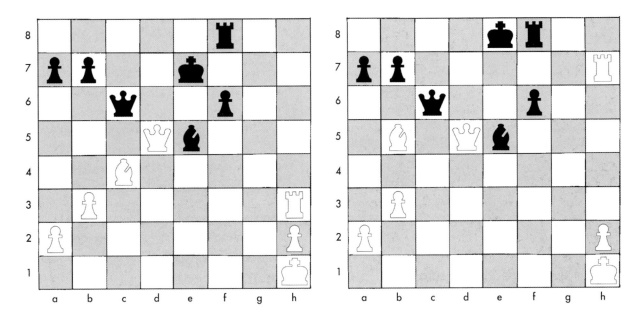

Fig 9. The White Rook is ready to fight back.

Fig 10. The White Bishop, protected by the White Queen, pins the helpless Black Queen.

White to move. White's Queen is Pinned against the King by the Black Queen and can't move. But the White Rook and Bishop are still on the loose. The Rook has a nasty plan (see Fig 9, above):

1. R h7 + !   K e8

2. B b5 (See Fig 10)

Black to move. Suddenly, White's Queen is no longer threatened by the Black Queen. The Black Queen is Pinned against the King by the White Bishop and can't move. White will win the Queen, thanks to the deadly Pin (see Fig 10, above).

The Fork

One of the most delightful ways of scaring the hell out of your opponent is to attack two of his pieces at the same time with just one of yours.

Of course, this situation is only of any use to you when neither of the pieces being attacked can capture the threatening piece.

One of the pieces can obviously run for safety on its next move.

But that doesn't help the other piece.

It'll be captured. And nothing can save it.

As we told you earlier on, one piece in particular is extremely adept at pulling off the Fork.

The Knight.

Because he has a unique way of moving, you won't always see what he's up to.

Until it's too late.

In Fig 1, the Black Knight seems to be much too far away from the White King and Queen to even warrant consideration.

In Fig 2, the Black Knight has made his move.

And he's now having a good laugh at the Queen's expense.

The White King has been Checked, and must use his next move to get out of Check.

There's nothing he can do for the White Queen except send her a wreath.

She'll be captured next move by the Knight.

On the following pages, you'll see more examples of the Fork, and how to set up Forking situations.

And you'll also discover that the Knight isn't the only piece capable of executing the Fork.

It's a lethal weapon.

Make sure you never miss a chance to use it.

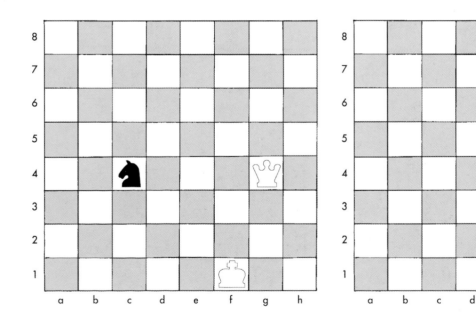

Fig 1. Surely the Black Knight can't do much damage here...

Fig 2. ...Well, wadda y'know? In one move, the White King has been Checked by the Knight, and his Queen is attacked as well. White's first priority is to get out of check. His Queen will be captured by the Knight next move.

White to move. By pushing his Pawn one square forward, White Checks the Black King and attacks the Black Queen all in one move. Black must somehow get out of Check. The King can't take the Pawn as that would immediately put him in Check from the Knight. If the Queen took the Pawn, she would be taken by the Knight. Black has problems. What would you do (see Fig 3, below)?

In one move the Bishop has Forked the King and the Rook. The Rook will be taken after the King has got himself out of Check (see Fig 4, below).

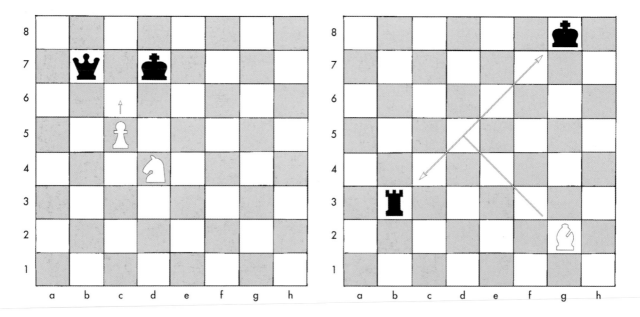

Fig 3. A classic Fork. The Queen is lost.

Fig 4. The Bishop will take the Rook after checking the Black King.

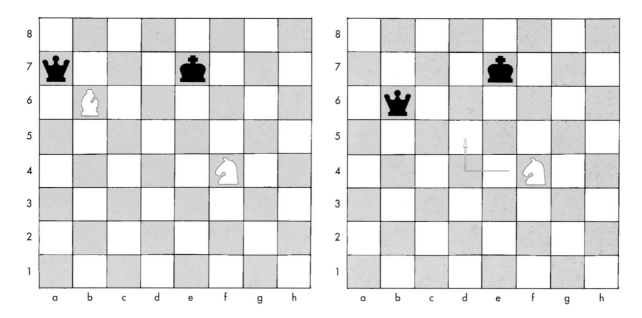

Fig 5. The White Bishop springs a trap.

Fig 6. The Knight has the King and the Queen at his mercy.

White to move. The White Bishop moves right into trouble from the
Black Queen (see Fig 5, above). It looks like an utterly senseless move.
In fact, it's a clever sacrifice. Look what happens in Fig 6.

The Black Queen gobbles up the White Bishop and falls right into
White's devilish little trap (see Fig 6, above). The Knight moves,
Checks the King and Forks the King and the Queen at the same time.
The Black Queen will be taken on White's next move.

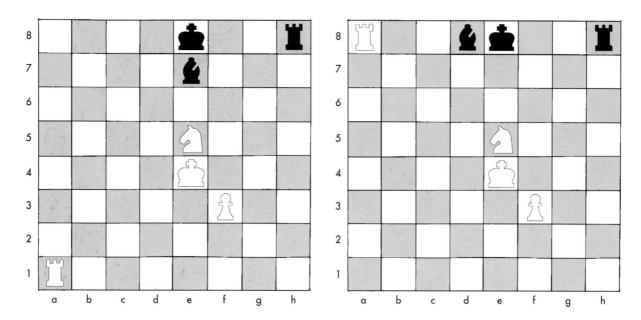

Fig 7. The White Rook has a plan.

Fig 8. The White Rook can now set up a Fork for his Knight.

White to move. White spots a Fork and begins to set it up.

1. R a8 + ! (see Fig 7, above).

Black can only relieve the Check by:

1. …B d8 followed by:

2. R x d8 + !   K x d8

3. N f7 + ! (Forking the King and the Rook.)

The Black Rook is lost, and White has won a Rook and Bishop in exchange for a Rook. Well worth it (see Fig 8, above).

White to move. White's Knight is Pinned by the Black Queen, so at the moment it cannot move. But he can pull off a Knight Fork with the startling

1. Q x d4 + !   Q x d4   (The Pin is broken). See Fig 9, below.

White to move.

2. N f5 + Forking the Black King and Queen. So White wins a Queen and a Knight, in exchange for a Queen. Powerful stuff (see Fig 10, below).

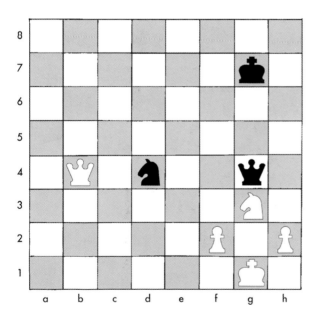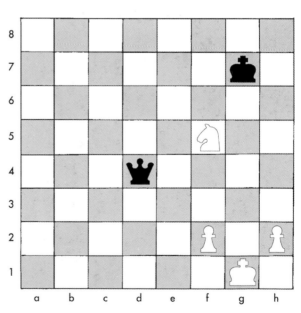

Fig 9. The White Queen is ready to free up its Knight.

Fig 10. The White Knight Forks the King and the Queen. The King is in check and the Queen is lost.

The Skewer

Picture if you will, the following little scene.

A man, standing some distance away from you, is about to shoot an arrow at you.

You are not alone. In fact, someone has very conveniently chosen to stand right in front of you.

You'd be forgiven for thinking that this person was providing a fair measure of protection.

But, naturally enough, he dislikes having arrows shot at him as much as you do.

And so this is what happens.

The man shoots the arrow.

And the person in front of you decides that he has little choice but to sidestep neatly out of its path.

Who stops the arrow?

Sorry about this, but you do.

In Chess, the very same set of circumstances is called the Skewer.

In Fig 1, the Black Queen is hiding behind the King. She thinks she's safe.

In fact, she's about as safe as a snowball in hell.

The White Bishop moves, Checks the Black King, and as you know, he must immediately get himself out of Check. Which he does by neatly sidestepping out of the line of fire, leaving his Queen at the mercy of the White Bishop.

As you will appreciate, the following rule is a good one to remember: KINGS ARE LOUSY AT SHIELDING MAJOR PIECES FROM ATTACK. Here's another one that works without the Check.

In Fig 2, it's Black to move.

The main consideration is the Black Queen. If she stayed where she was and moved the Rook instead, she'd be taken next move by the White Bishop.

Or, if she took the white Bishop, she'd be taken next move by the White Pawn, losing out on the swap.

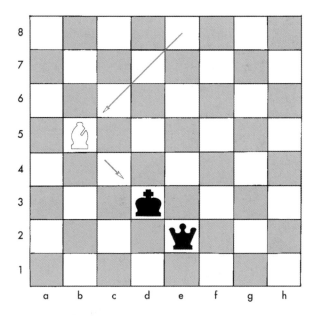

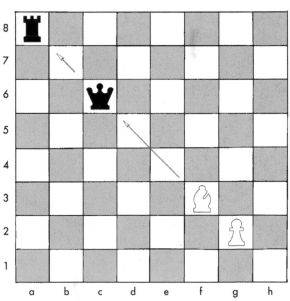

Fig 1. The White Bishop moves, and Checks the Black King. Whatever the King chooses to do to get himself out of Check, he will leave his Queen at the mercy of the Bishop. And as you know, mercy is not one of the Bishop's strongest points.

Fig 2. Black to move. After considering all her possible moves, the Queen will reluctantly decide to save herself and sidestep away from the Bishop's attack. The Rook behind her is left to die.

So she has little choice but to save herself, and sidestep neatly out of the line of fire. A move the Black Rook will not like in the slightest.

Remember, the object of the Skewer is TO FORCE AN ENEMY PIECE OUT OF THE WAY SO YOU CAN GET AT ANOTHER PIECE HIDING BEHIND IT. You can't wait to try it out, can you?

White to move. The White Rook spots a possible Skewer. And here's how he sets it up:
1. R x d4 +   K x d4 (see Fig 3, below).

…and suddenly two of Black's major pieces are lying in a straight line on the same Diagonal!
2. B f2 + ! And the King must move out of the way, leaving the Rook behind him a sitting duck. The Bishop will take the Rook next move (see Fig 4, below).

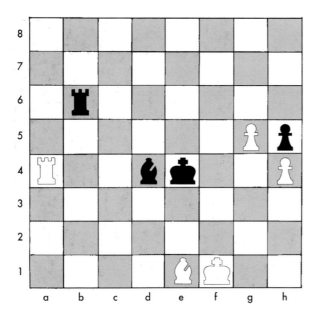

Fig 3. The White Rook spots a skewer.

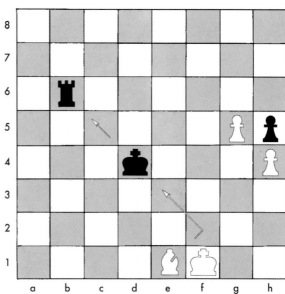

Fig 4. The White Bishop finishes it off by checking on f2 before taking the Black Rook.

Black to move. Here, Black sets up a Skewer from nothing. And here's
how he does it (see Fig 5, below):

1. ...R x f3 +

2. K x f3 (see Fig 6, below)

Now look. The White King and Rook are lying on the same Diagonal.
Absolutely begging to be Skewered. And they get what they're asking for.

2. ...B g4 + ! The King must move out of the way, leaving the Rook at
the mercy of the Black Bishop. He will be taken next move.

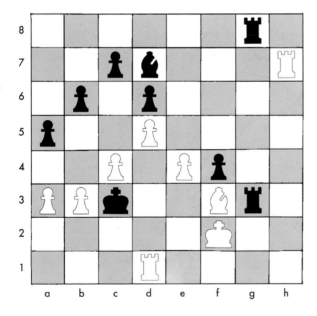

Fig 5. The Black Rook is about to take the
White Bishop on F3. Check.

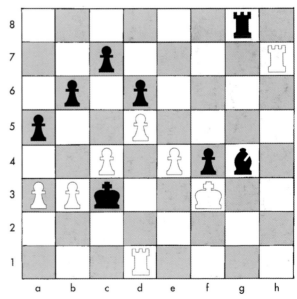

Fig 6. When the White King moves out of Check,
the White Rook will be taken.

White to move (see Fig 7, below). The White Queen wouldn't take the Black Queen, because she would in turn be taken by the Black King. So instead, White conjures up a nasty little Skewer (see Fig 8, below).

1. R h7 +

The Black Rook can block the attack by …R f7, but if you play that out you'll see why Black loses out all round.

1. R x f7 +   …K x f7
2. Q x d7 +
The Skewer has won the day.

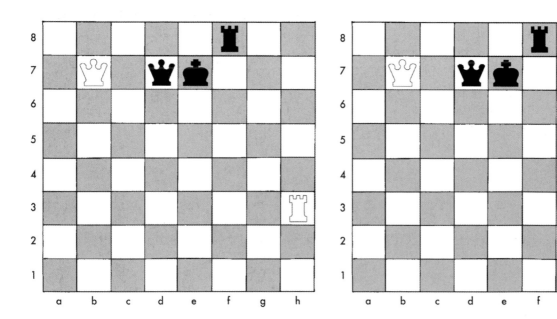

Fig 7. The White Rook is ready to move.   **Fig 8.** By a Check on h7 he creates a nasty Skewer that wins the day.

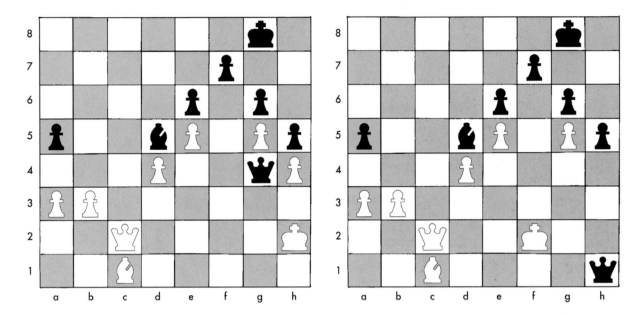

Fig 9. The Black Queen is ready to pounce. **Fig 10.** The Black queen can now complete the Skewer.

Black to move (see Fig 9, above). Black could make a Check with his Queen at g2. But the White Queen could easily dispose of this threat. So Black must get rid of the White Queen, and he does so with a stylish Skewer.

1.   ...Q x h4 +
2.   K g1   Q h1 +
3.   K f2   (See Fig 10, above)

Black to move (see Fig 9, above). Black has now forced the White King and Queen on to the same Rank. Here comes the Skewer:

3. ...Q h2 + !

The King must move out of the way, leaving his Queen in a fatal position. Instant Divorce.

The Discovered Attack

Once upon a time there was a nice little old lady selling flowers out of a nice little old basket.

Now, this basket had a lid on it. But it was safe to assume that it was full of flowers because there were a few blooms poking out of the top.

After a while, a man came up and asked if he could see inside the basket as he wanted very much to buy some of her flowers. She said he would be welcome, and opened the lid.

{It's not funny out there – someone just got mugged!}

Inside, instead of flowers, was a note which read as follows: DON'T MOVE OR I'LL PLUG YOU. I HAVE A .38 UNDER MY DRESS.

Surprise, surprise.

The little old lady was a mugger. And not only that, she was a master of the Discovered Attack. Let us show you how the Discovered Attack works in Chess.

In Fig 1, it's White to move. The two enemy Queens are on the same Rank, but they can't get at each other, because the White Bishop is in the way.

Well, at least that's what it looks like at first glance. Watch this. The White Bishop takes the lid off the situation by capturing the Black Pawn and Checking the Black King.

Not only that, he unmasks an attack on the Black Queen by the White Queen.

Unfortunately, Black must use his next move to get out of Check. (Remember that rule). And the White Queen captures the Black Queen with no trouble at all next move.

Set the pieces up as they are in the diagram, and play that move through.

It's one of the basic patterns of the Discovered Attack.

To put the whole thing in a nutshell, here's the principle of the Discovered Attack.

BY MOVING ONE OF YOUR OWN PIECES INTO A DIRECT ATTACKING POSITION, YOU ALSO UNMASK A CLEAR ATTACKING OPPORTUNITY FOR ONE OF YOUR PIECES BEHIND IT OR BESIDE IT.

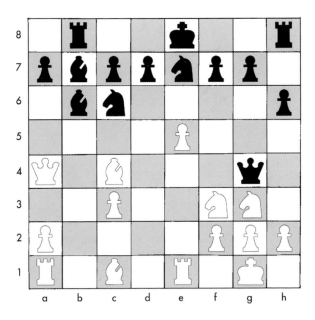

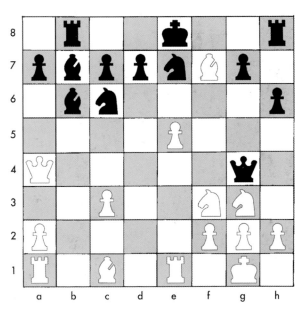

Fig 1. White to move. By taking the Black Pawn on f7, the White Bishop Checks the Black King. And that's not all he does. He gives the White Queen a clear view of the Black Queen.

Fig 2. The Black King must use his next move to get out of Check. Which he does by taking the White Bishop. The Bishop didn't die for nothing. His Queen can now take the Black Queen.

The Discovered Check

This nasty little piece of business is based on exactly the same idea as the Discovered Attack.

Only this time, instead of unmasking an attack from one of your own pieces, you unmask a Check.

Check? OK – we'll go and tell the king

In Fig 1 The White Rook is aching to swing a punch at the Black King. But he can't for the moment, because the White Knight is in the way.

Now, the White Knight knows that any move he makes will unmask a Check on the Black King by the White Rook. So he searches round for the move that will cause the most panic.

It's not very difficult to spot the right move for the Knight to make. In Fig 2 you see where he went.

Let's analyze it. First of all, his move unmasked a Check on the Black King by the White Rook.

Second, you'll notice that the Knight is in a position to take the Black Queen next move.

So what happens?

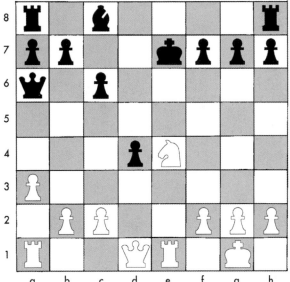

Fig 1. Any move the White Knight makes will give the White Rook a Discovered Check on the Black King.

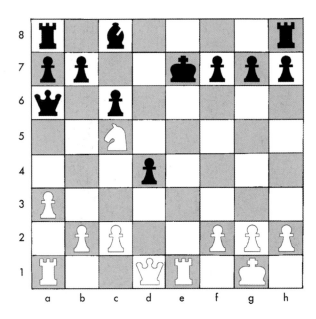

Fig 2. Cool as you like, the Knight moves, attacks the Black Queen, and at the same time gives his Rook a clear sight of the Black King. The King must use his next move to get out of Check. Leaving his Queen to the White Knight. Who will have his way with her.

The Black King has no alternative but to forget his Queen's predicament, to get out of Check immediately. We don't have to tell you what the White Knight then does to the Black Queen.

Our advice on the subject of Discovered Attacks and Checks is to keep an eye open for them all the time. They can do a great deal of damage.

Also, watch out for little old ladies selling flowers.

For the same reason.

The Double Attack

One day soon, you'll find yourself sitting opposite an opponent who eats rookie Chess players for breakfast. And you'll soon discover that this kind of person has absolutely no sense of fair play whatsoever.

He'll play dirty and rough. Which, as you know, is in the best traditions of the game.

He'll probably know every trick in the book.

One of these tricks will almost certainly be the Double Attack. It's a real pig.

For your own safety, we strongly advise you to learn it.

At first glance, the Double Attack looks very much like the Discovered Attack. But there's a subtle difference.

In one charming little move, you can unleash two attacks on one enemy piece at the same time.

In Fig 1, it's White to move. The White Rook, the White Bishop and the Black Queen are all in a straight line on the same File.

This is the first sign that something nasty is about to happen. It does. (See Fig 2).

The White Bishop moves to attack the Queen.

At the same time, he's left the White Rook with a clear view of the Black Queen.

In one move, the Black Queen has suddenly been attacked from two different directions.

Of course, the Queen could capture either Bishop or Rook. But they're both defended by a Pawn, so she doesn't.

She has no alternative but to run for cover.

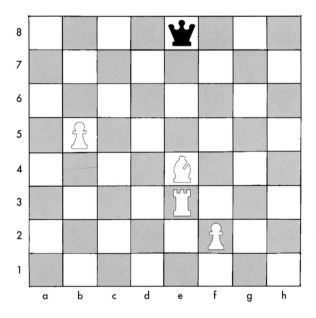

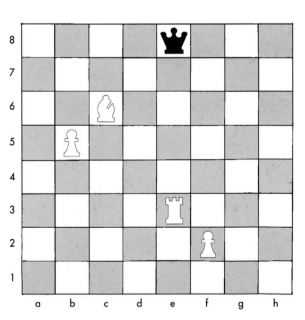

Fig 1. If the White Bishop moved, the Rook behind him could attack the Black Queen. If the White Bishop could move to a square where he would also be attacking the Queen, that would be even better. Where does he go?

Fig 2. c6. The Pawn will protect him. And the Black Queen finds herself being attacked from two different directions after just one move.

The Double Check

Exactly the same as the Double Attack, only this time instead of attacking an enemy piece from two directions, you put the enemy King in Check from two different directions.

In Fig 1, it's the Black King we're after as opposed to the Black Queen.

In Fig 2, the White Bishop makes the same move as before, Checking the King from one direction, and unmasking a Check by the White Rook from another.

The King can't move any of his own pieces to block the Double Check.

He only has one alternative.

Flee. 'My Kingdom for a horse.'

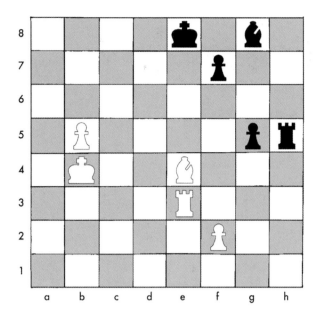

Fig 1. The Black King is in the wrong place at the wrong time. The White Bishop is ready to move.

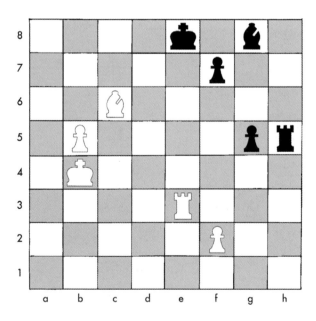

Fig 2. The Black King now finds himself in check by two pieces, the Bishop and the Rook.

THE WHOLE SHOOTING MATCH FROM START TO FINISH

If you ever hear an average Chess player say that he operates with a long-term strategical plan in mind, he's either trying to scare you, or he's lying through his teeth.

It would be fair to say that the only players who can successfully carry out a long-term plan of attack are big-time tournament players.

Their powers of concentration are immense.

And they don't scare too easily.

Of course, this doesn't mean to say that playing tactically from one move to the next is a bad thing.

So long as you think you know what you're supposed to be doing, and you have a few nasty tricks up your sleeve as well, you'll get along just fine. And you'll have a lot of fun.

Hopefully, it won't be too long before you're thinking up to three or four moves ahead. And don't forget, that won't do you any good unless you've worked out your opponent's best moves as well.

But there are certain stages of the game that you should be familiar with, where pretty much the same conditions crop up time and time again.

And there are some basic tips that we can give you, that will help you build up some idea of how you're going to cope with them and humiliate your opponent.

Not surprisingly, these stages are called:
1. The Opening.
2. The Middle Game.
3. The Endgame.

Here is a broad picture of the battle from start to finish.

The Opening

The main idea behind the Opening is to get your pieces out as quickly and sensibly as possible. At this stage of the game you shouldn't be thinking about killing.

You should be concentrating on building a strong position IN THE CENTRE OF THE BOARD.

If you start messing around at the sides of the board, YOU WILL LOSE. And that's a fact.

Standard Openings

As a beginner, one of the first things you should do is learn a standard Opening.

And there are plenty to choose from. Some are named after the key pieces they involve, and others after the man who created them.

Some are a lot bolder than others, needing a lot of precision to make them pay off.

Forget those for the time being. Play out the two examples we're about to show you, and learn them backwards. They're both very simple.

A word of advice. Although these are very common opening moves, and good to be familiar with, don't go following them blindly if your opponent is, for example, about to capture your Queen!

No matter how much you know about Chess, it's what's taking place on the board that you have to worry about.

The Giuoco Piano opening

This one wasn't invented by Mr. G. Piano.

In Italian, *Giuoco Piano* means 'quiet game'. It leads to a very sound deployment of pieces on both sides, but because nothing very dramatic happens, neither side gains any real advantage early on.

You can see how it looks in Fig 1. Incidentally, you should study this opening from Black's point of view as well as White's.

Play it out and see how we got to this quiet position.

WHITE	BLACK
1. e4	e5
2. N f3	N c6
3. B c4	B c5
4. N c3	N f6
5. d3	d6
6. B e3	B b6
7. Q d2	B e6
8. B b3	Q d7
9. O – O – O	O – O – O (Queen-side)

As you can see, both the White and Black positions are identical. White might try to open things up by swapping both Bishops. What would you do?

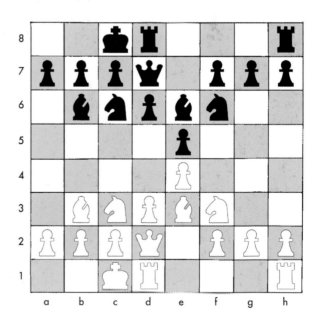

Fig 1. The Giuoco Piano Opening.

The Four Knights opening

Named after the Four Knights who play a big part in it. Once again, very nice deployment of pieces, but nothing dramatic, and so no real advantage for White. But a good solid beginning.

WHITE	BLACK
1. e4	e5
2. N f3	N c6
3. N c3	N f6
4. B b5	B b4
5. O – O	O – O (King-side)
6. d3	d6
7. B g5	B x c3
8. b x c3	

If you're fortunate enough to be playing White, you'll be making the first move of the battle. (As White always does).

So for a time, you'll have a slight advantage over your opponent because you'll be calling the tune.

It's very important that you should hang on to this advantage for as long as possible.

Here are a few tips to help you do this:

1. Never, if possible, move the same piece more than once during the Opening. It will waste a valuable opportunity to get some of your other pieces on the move.

2. Never move a piece to a position that it will obviously have to move away from next move. This will also waste precious time.

3. Make sure that the pieces you've advanced have enough protection. If they have, your opponent won't bother to attack them. This again will give you time to get on with the job.

As soon as your opponent finds a way of making you retreat during the Opening, you'll have lost that precious one-move advantage and the situation will be even.

In Chess Lingo, this is called 'Losing Tempo'. Not to be confused with losing your temper.

If you're playing Black, exactly the same things apply. Only this time, you'll be concentrating on never falling more than one move behind.

Now, here are some general tips:

1. Always open with a centre Pawn. Either the King's Pawn or the Queen's Pawn. Never even consider opening with a Pawn on the edge of the board.

2. If you're playing Black, and White kicks off with 1. e4, REPLY WITH e5 YOURSELF. (Later on, you'll discover other replies to 1. e4).

3. Don't make unnecessary Pawn moves. Remember, they can never retreat.

4. Get your Knights out first, and then your Bishops. Leave the Rooks and the Queen till later.

5. Castle early. As we explained earlier, this will get one of your Rooks moving, and tuck your King away at the same time.

6. Don't go rushing off with your Queen trying to win the war single-handed. Every army marches on its stomach. Supply lines must be kept open, and reinforcements must always be at the ready. It takes a team to win a war.

7. Check every move carefully before you make it. Bad blunders early on are difficult to make up for.

8. Use your brain. It can always do with a little exercise.

9. There's only one Golden Rule. And that is, there are no Golden Rules. Inspiration is half the battle.

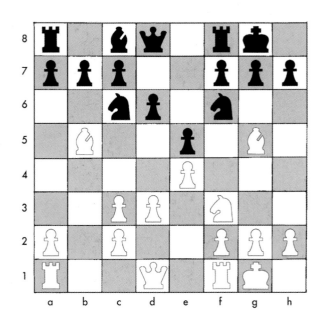

Fig 2. The Four Knights Opening.

The Middle Game

After the Opening comes the Middle Game. To be perfectly honest, the battlefield at this stage of the game is one big scrimmage.

The centre of the board is usually crowded with pieces, face to face, with neither side in a hurry to take the initiative.

And this is where you really have to use your head.

The problem is, both sides have deployed their pieces into very similar positions and room to move about in is hard to find. (You could of course start moving backwards, but that would be pointless).

The only way to make room and start advancing is by capturing enemy pieces.

But they're all very well defended, so what's the answer?

First of all, you must remember that the player who wins more pieces, or more powerful pieces than his opponent, usually turns out to be the winner.

So the trick is to start making room by trading pieces as long as you don't lose out on the deal.

For instance, don't capture an enemy Knight with a Rook if it means losing that Rook next move in the process.

Exchange a Knight for a Knight. A Bishop for a Bishop and so on.

There is only one exception to this rule. The deliberate sacrifice.

Sometimes, you'll be smart enough to see that exchanging one of your big pieces for one of your opponent's little pieces will be well worth it in the end because it clears the way for a real razzmatazz thrust you've got planned for your next move.

This will be very unnerving for your opponent. On one hand he'll have a golden opportunity to gobble up one of your major pieces so easily it looks like you've blundered. But on the other hand he'll be thinking 'This is too good to be true. What's the rat got up his sleeve now?'

Watching your opponent sweat and squirm at times like this makes the whole game worthwhile, even if you wind up losing.

But naturally, the most efficient way of wearing down your opponent is to figure out ways of toppling his big pieces with your small pieces.

Now for some general tips:

1. Try to think ahead, but not too far ahead. You can't always anticipate what the enemy is going to do next.

2. Don't allow him to capture one of your pieces unless you can capture an equally valuable piece in return.

3. Take a good long look at the square you're planning to move one of your pieces to. Satisfy yourself that the square isn't guarded by an enemy piece.

4. Take a good long look at all the enemy pieces lined up against you. Make sure none of your pieces will be captured by any of them next move. If any of them will be, do something about it.

5. Start looking for Pins, Forks and Skewering possibilities.
   THE TIME IS RIPE.

6. Don't worry too much about making dreadful mistakes. There's no better way to learn.

The Endgame

Assuming that both players have been clever enough to survive the Middle Game, they will come to the Endgame.

A situation where the last tired remnants of each army battle it out till they drop.

Many beginners think that because there are very few pieces left on the board, the final kill will come quickly and cleanly.

This just isn't the case.

Certainly, there's plenty of room for attacking pieces to sweep around in.

But it works both ways.

There's plenty of room for the hounded Kings to dodge about in.

It can often take an infuriatingly long time for an inexperienced player to corner the enemy King.

Assuming your opponent is left only with his King, you must AT LEAST have the following pieces to be able to Checkmate him. Otherwise, CHECKMATE WILL BE PHYSICALLY IMPOSSIBLE.

1. A King and a Queen.
2. A King and a Rook.
3. A King, a Knight and a Bishop. (Only if the enemy King is in a corner square commanded by your Bishop.)
4. A King and both Bishops.
5. A King, a Knight and a Pawn. (Assuming the Pawn can be promoted.)
6. A King, a Bishop and a Pawn. (Assuming the Pawn can be promoted.)
7. A King and a Pawn. (Assuming the Pawn can be promoted.)
8. A King and 2 Knights can Mate only if the King is stupid enough to get himself into the corner. (But in most games it usually ends in a draw.)

A KING AND A KNIGHT AGAINST A LONE KING IS A DRAW.

SO IS A KING AND A BISHOP AGAINST A LONE KING.

Try it now and see for yourself.

Finally, remember the rule that says two Kings must never be on adjacent squares.

This may not mean much during the Opening and Middle Game. But in the Endgame, it's vitally important.

Good luck. And may the biggest thug win.

Combinations. The old One-two.

What's better than one nasty trick? Three nasty tricks in a row.

For the second time in this book, we'd like you to imagine two gentlemen in a boxing ring trying to render each other unconscious.

Both are attempting to out-guess the other with a variety of fairly simple tactics.

One way of bringing the fight to a sudden end is the big knockout punch.

Bam. And it's all over.

The other way is slightly more subtle.

It involves maybe three punches in quick succession. A left to the body, a right to the body, at which point the unfortunate gentleman will very likely go weak at the knees, double up in pain, and remember nothing about the wicked uppercut that collided with his face a split second later.

In boxing, this is called a combination.

In Chess, it's also called a combination. For the very same reasons.

To go back to that flurry of punches for a moment, you'll appreciate that once the two

punches had arrived at their target on the midriff, it was a foregone conclusion that he was going to double up.

To look at it another way, he was FORCED TO DOUBLE UP.

Softening him up for the final killer punch.

In Chess, you can very often do the same thing.

By stringing together a wicked combination of moves, YOU CAN FORCE YOUR OPPONENT TO DO EXACTLY WHAT YOU WANT HIM TO DO.

This obviously makes life a lot easier for you.

Instead of having to guess what your opponent is going to do next, you know EXACTLY what he's going to do next.

This is called A FORCED RESPONSE, for obvious reasons.

We now show a few examples of this very unfriendly behaviour.

Play them out now, and waste no time in practising them on your best friends.

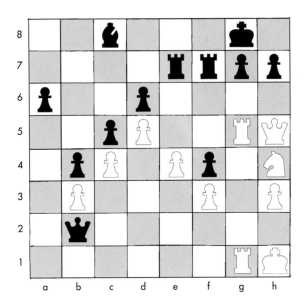

The Black Queen pays dearly for wandering away from the battle. White to move.

1. Q x h7 + ! K x h7
2. R h5 + K g8
3. N g6 R f6
4. R h8 + K f7
5. R f8 # ! Checkmate!

Jazz wasn't the only good thing to come out of New Orleans. In the mid 19th century, the city produced a child Chess prodigy. His name was Paul Morphy. Here is one of his delightful little combinations.

White to move.

1. R f8 + Q x f8
2. R x f8 + R x f8
3. Q x g6 # ! Checkmate!

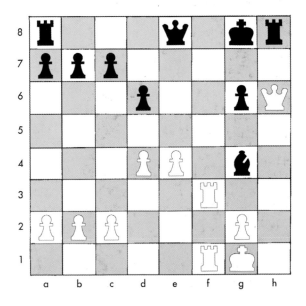

Akiba Rubinstein would have probably won the World Chess Championship had it not been for an even bigger battle, the First World War.

Here he uses a sneaky Rook up his King side. Black to move.

1. …   Q x h2 + !
2. K x h2   h4 x g3 + !
3. K g1   R h1 # Checkmate

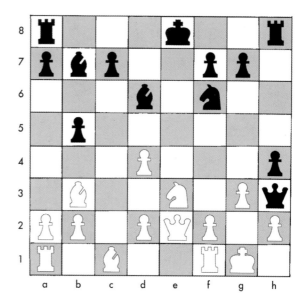

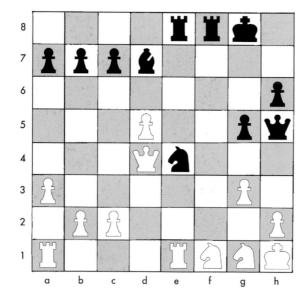

Aron Nimzovitsch was one of the great players of the 1920s.

Here we see Nimzovitsch put White on the rack. Black to move.

1. …   N f2 +
2. K g2   B h3 +
3. N x h3   Q f3 +
4. K g1   N x h3 # Checkmate

The White King is cornered.

Black's got an extra Rook, but White's got the big ideas. White to move.

1. R x c6 + !   Q x c6
2. Q b4 # Checkmate

Brave and bold.

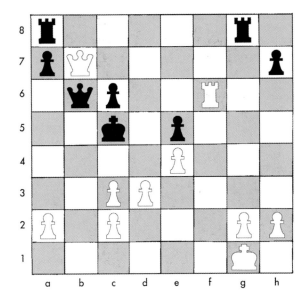

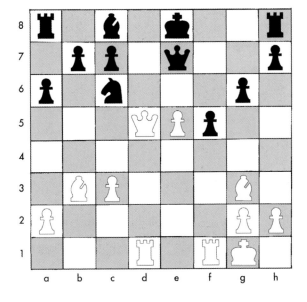

Black's Queen just can't cope.
White to move.

1. B h4 !   Q g7

(The Queen can't take the White Bishop, because of the threat of Q f7 #)

2. Q d8 + !   N x d8
3. R x d8 # Checkmate

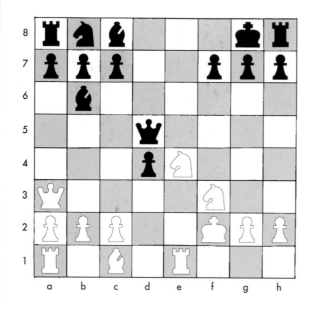

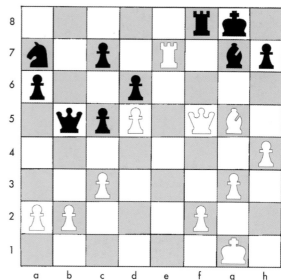

Black's pieces are in all the wrong places.
White to move.

1. N f6 + !   g x f6
2. Q f8 + !   K x f8
3. B h6 +   K g8
4. R e8 # Checkmate

What a way to sacrifice a Queen! Brilliant.

Cracks appear in Black's defence.
White to move.

1. R x g7 + !   K x g7
2. B h6 + !   K x h6
3. Q g5 # Checkmate

Even though he has more pieces, White's in
trouble. And Black knows it.
Black to move.

1. ...   Q f1 + !
2. R g1   N g3 + !
3. h x g3   Q h3 # Checkmate

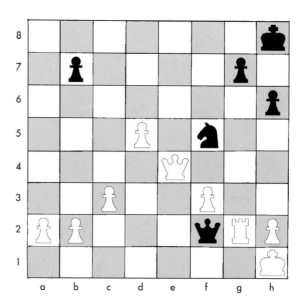

A Bishop down, Black pulls off the impossible.
The White Queen is stranded.
Black to move.

1. …	Q f1 + !
2. B g1	Q f3 + !!
3. B x f3	B x f3 # Checkmate

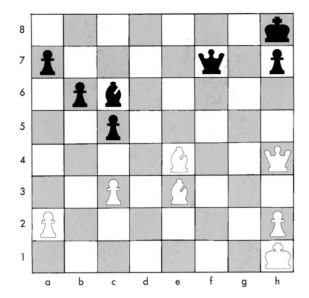

AND THAT CONCLUDES THE SECTION ON VIOLENCE AND SUDDEN DEATH.

Wasn't it nice?

Six tasty little battles that might help you win a few of your own.

Play them out now.

It's worth it.

Ruy Lopez: An 8-move game

WHITE	BLACK
1. e4	e5
2. N f3	N c6
3. B b5	N d4
4. B c4	B c5
5. N x e5 ?	…
See Fig 1	

White thinks he's ahead, but in fact, he's blown it.

5. …	Q g5
6. N x f7	Q x g2
7. R f1	Q x e4 +
8. B e2	N f3 # Checkmate

The White King can't move.

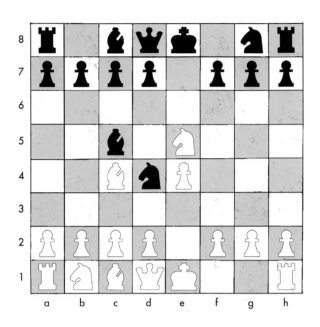

Fig 1. White isn't ahead, he's in trouble.

King's Gambit: A 12-move game

Black wins a few Pawns, but loses the game.

WHITE	BLACK
1. e4	e5
2. f4	e x f4
3. N f3	B e7
4. B c4	B h4 +
5. g 3 ! ?	f x g3
6. O – O	g x h2 +
7. K h1	B e7 ?

See Fig 2.

8. B x f7 +	K x f7
9. N e5 +	K e6
10. Q g4 +	K x e5
11. Q f5 +	K d6
12. Q d5 # Checkmate	

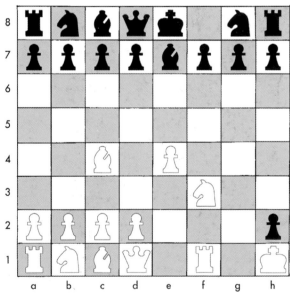

Fig 2. The Black King and Queen are
hemmed in by their Bishop.

New Orleans 1849

3 This is a short game between the precocious 12-year-old Paul Morphy and his father, Alonzo Morphy. By the age of twenty, Paul had become one of the greatest Chess players the world has ever seen.

Play it out now and watch young Paul take his old man apart.

Fig 1. The Black Bishop is tempted to take a loose Pawn.

PAUL MORPHY	ALONZO MORPHY
1. e4	e5
2. N f3	N c6
3. B c4	B c5
4. b4	See Fig 1

Young Paul wants the centre. He's prepared to give a Pawn to get it.

4. …	B x b4
5. c3	B c5
6. d4	e x d4
7. c x d4	B b6
8. O – O	N a5
9. B d3	d5 ?
10. e x d5	Q x d5
11. B a3 !	B e6
12. N c3	Q d7
13. d5	…

Paul offers a Pawn to his Dad. Whether or not he takes it, Paul will get a wicked Check on the King File.

13. …	B x d5
14. N x d5	Q x d5
15. B b5 + !!	…

A beautiful move, especially from a twelve-year-old. Black must capture because if … 15. … c6, Paul replies with Q x d5 and Alonzo cannot capture Paul's Queen in return.

15. ...	Q x b5
16. R e1 +	N e7
17. R b1 ? !	...

Paul gets a little too excited. And gives Black a chance to make a fight
of it with … 17. … Q d7, 18. R x e7 +, Q x e7, 19. B x e7, K x e7 etc.

17. ...	Q a6
18. R x e7 +	...

Now young Paul is on the right track again.

18. ...	K f8
19. Q d5	Q c4
20. R x f7 +	K g8
21. R f8 # mate (sorry Dad…)	

A particularly nasty Discovered Double Check provides
a beautiful finish.

Youth is a wonderful thing.

The old man bites the dust.

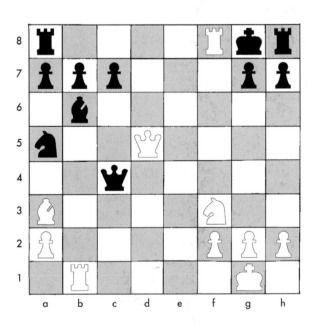

Fig 2. The Black King is left horribly exposed. Checkmate.

Fischer v. Spassky 1972

The collapse of the Soviet Union probably started in 1972 with the American Bobby Fischer winning the World Chess Championship with a decisive victory over Boris Spassky in Reykjavik.

This win finally broke the stranglehold that Russia had held in international Chess.

His 12.5 to 8.5 triumph changed the world of Chess forever.

The cold war starts to hot up. See Fig 1.

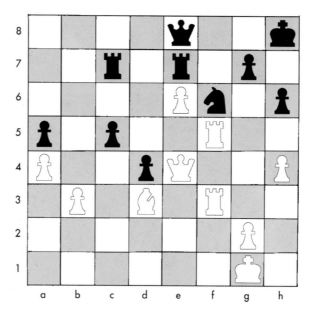

Fig 1. Fischer is about to turn up the heat.

Fischer, playing White, surprises Spassky yet again with:

38. R x f6 !	g x f6
39. R x f6	K g8
40. B c4	K h8
41. Q f4	...

Bobby has Boris in a pickle. His war is nearly over.

5 Kasparov v. Hracek 1996

White to move. See Fig 2.

22. B x d5 !   B d7
23. Rh e1   h6
24. f x e6   f x e6
25. Q a7

Kasparov opens up with more body blows.
Hracek's hands are starting to drop as Gary now
threatens to move in for the kill with B x e6.

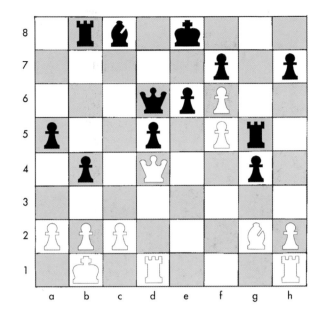

Fig 2. Kasparov has a surprise for Hracek.

6 Kasparov v. Topalov 1999

Topalov has fought a tough rearguard
action but Kasparov has more tricks up his sleeve
than Rasputin. See Fig 3.

37 R d7 !   R x d7
38. B x c4   b x c4
39. Q x h8   R d3
40. Q a8   c3
41. Q a4 +   K e1
42. f4   f5
43. K c1   R d2
44. Q a7   Black resigns himself to defeat.

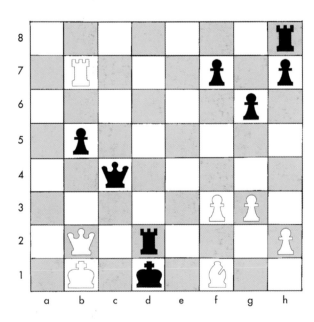

Fig 3. Kasparov finds an inventive attacking move…

Without solutions there wouldn't be any problems.

If you enjoy solving problems and pondering over puzzles, Chess provides an Aladdin's Cave of possibilities. Newspapers, books and magazines are an unending source of mysteries to exercise your brain.

Here are a few to cut your teeth on and get you battle hardened for the challenges ahead.

Answers buried at the end of the book.

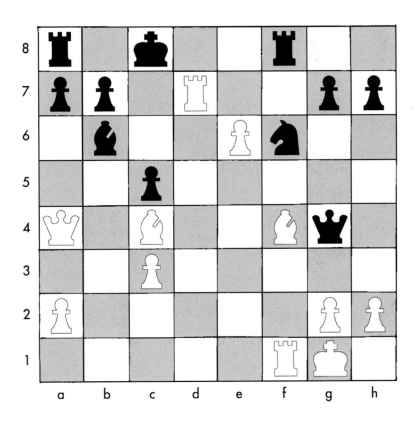

Morphy – Thompson, New York 1859.

White to move.

A characteristic swashbuckling finish by Paul Morphy.

How does he finish off Black?

(Answer on page 142)

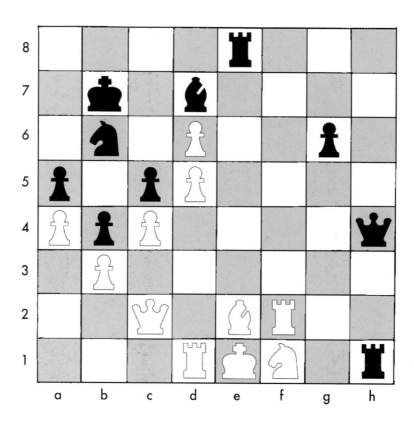

Kovacevic – Seirawan, Wijk aan Zee 1980.

Black to move.

Can you spot Black's decisive attack?

(Answer on page 142)

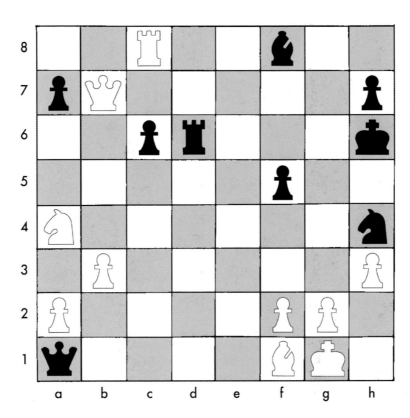

Van der Sterren – Kamsky, Wijk aan Zee 1994.

Black to move.

Although the Black King is exposed, the White King's Pawns provide little protection. How does Black exploit White's position?

(Answer on page 142)

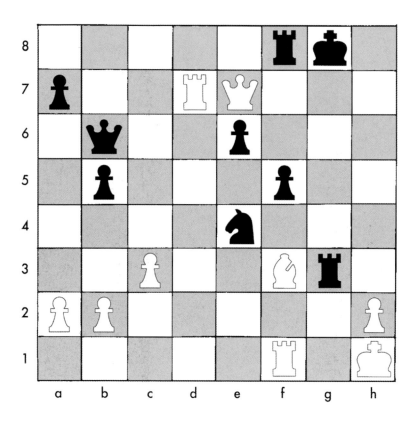

A classic finish

Black has his back to the wall and White is about to mate. But great players make things happen. How does Black turn the tables?

(Answer on page 142)

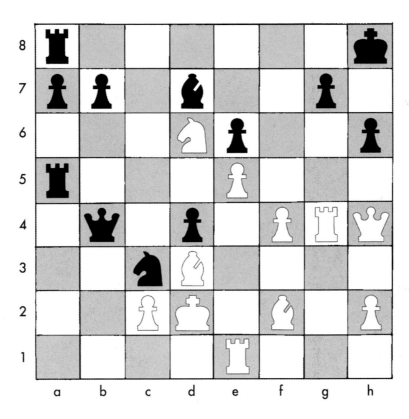

Fischer – Benko, Curaçao 1962.

White to move.

White seems to be in all kinds of trouble. Fischer needs a life-saving flash of brilliance. What was it?

(Answer on page 142)

For us this is the end. For you, it's just the beginning.

By this stage, you've probably played a few games of Chess and discovered a bunch of muscles in your brain you never knew existed.

You've probably also discovered how absolutely rotten it feels to lose and how immensely satisfying it can be to carry out a little plan of attack and win.

If that's the case, we couldn't have hoped for more. Because that's what Chess is all about.

But make no mistake. You've barely scratched the surface. There's a whole new world of Chess goodies out there waiting to be discovered.

You can join Chess clubs and bang heads with top players.

You can try solving infuriating little Chess problems every day in most national newspapers.

You can follow World Championships and understand what the fuss is all about.

You can even get lost in the middle of Tibet knowing that, if nothing else, someone will be only too happy to give you a quick beating before the police show up and deport you.

But perhaps the most exciting development in Chess is the Internet. Even a mouse can play. Log into any Chess room you can find (there are loads of them), and you'll find literally thousands of other addicts playing online at any time of the night and day. This is a blast.

Playing someone you don't have to look at is a unique opportunity to torture a fellow human being.

And no one will ever find out.

Yes, people, Chess is the biggest thing to hit the Planet Earth, and we can prove it.

When Elvis was born, the game was already 5000 years old.

Play it, study it, read about it. And get your kids worked up about it too.

The way the little dears seem to pick things up so annoyingly quickly, who knows, one day you may be saying 'My son or daughter, the Chess player…'

Answers

These are the answers to the problems on pages 136–141.

Morphy v. Thompson, New York 1859.

1 Qc6+! bxc6 2 Ba6 mate

Kovacevic v. Seirawan, Wijk aan Zee 1980.

1 ... Rxf1+! 2 Kxf1 Qh1 mate

Van der Sterren v. Kamsky, Wijk aan Zee 1994.

1 ... Nf3+! 2 gxf3 Rg6+ forces mate

A classic finish

1 ... Qg1+! 2 Rxg1 Nf2 mate

Fischer v. Benko, Curaçao 1962.

1 Qxh6+! gxh6 2 Nf7 mate

The End

Index